ENDORSEMENTS

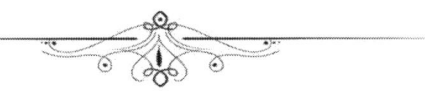

God speaks today! He speaks in many ways to His people. Prophecy is a gift that we are to pursue and esteem. Dr. Luc Niebergall has given us fantastic insights into the prophetic ministry of today. Each chapter is loaded with glory and revelation. You won't want to stop after the first page, for you were *Born to Hear God*. Get this book and get another copy to share with a friend. They will thank you for it!

- **Dr. Brian Simmons**
The Passion Translation
Passion and Fire Ministries

God is raising up prophetic reformers in this hour, and there is no doubt that Dr. Luc Niebergall is one of these dread champions, a leader, and a prophetic voice. In this book, *Born to Hear God*, Luc brings great insight into the various ways God speaks, unpacks revelation on the foundation of Scripture, and imparts practical tools. He does this while bringing a fresh perspective regarding the prophetic function through his own personal odyssey with God. *Born to Hear God* takes you into deeper waters and stirs your spirit to connect with the Father as He has always intended. This book will unlock the prophetic reformer within you. I highly recommend this book!

- **Tony Kim**
Executive Director of *Harvest International Ministry*

Whenever Holy Spirit is involved with a project, I always notice two things: It is simple, and yet at the same time profound. I observed this when I read Dr. Luc Niebergall's book *Born to Hear God*. Timeless prophetic principles are articulated openly and clearly yet carry a profound impact. There is something here for beginners, as well as those who have moved in prophetic ministry for years. What I enjoyed the most was story after story of encounters with God and real-life people whose lives were forever changed by the *rhema* word! This book can be the prelude to your own prophetic adventure with God! Enjoy!

- Dennis Wiedrick
Author of *A Royal Priesthood*

What a powerful, timely, and comprehensive book this is! *Born to Hear God* is a tool kit for the prophetic that will position every believer to better hear God's heart and heaven's strategic revelation with razor-sharp clarity.

Dr. Luc Niebergall is anointed to unlock and impart breakthrough in the prophetic, and you will discover biblically sound keys that will impact your call and circumstances. These pages contain practical mentoring and activations—but more than this—they will propel you into acceleration of all God is saying to you in this season. As Dr. Luc writes, "You truly are fashioned to hear the voice of the Lord," and this book will help you do just that... comprehend, accurately interpret, and apply the necessary voice of the King in your own life. I bless you as you read and commune with the God who speaks and is unlocking supernatural increase in your prophetic journey.

- Jodie Hughes
Pour it Out Ministries
pouritout.org
Revivalist, TV Host, Evangelist
Author of *The King's Decree* and *The King's Prophetic Voice*

We were created to hear the voice of God. It is in the very DNA of every believer to hear God and to respond. In *Born to*

Hear God, Dr. Luc Niebergall has laid out a path to help equip the everyday believer to understand that they can hear God's voice. In fact, no one can come to a living relationship with Jesus without first hearing Him. The Holy Spirit guided you to Jesus, and the Holy Spirit is still speaking. When God speaks, He will never contradict the written Word of God. I am excited as you go through such a practical guide to discovering how God is speaking and how He wants to speak to you. You were born to hear and respond in faith to the leading and guiding of the Spirit of God.

- Chris Overstreet
Compassion to Action

As a church planter/pastor and prophetic minister, I am constantly searching for biblical, accurate resources with church history that encourage community and challenge the reader to grow a more profound friendship with God. Dr. Luc Niebergall's book, *Born to Hear God*, is critical for those new to discovering the voice of God and those who have dove deep into the supernatural ministry. Topics such as *The Heart of the Prophetic* and *Prophetic Pitfalls* build a solid foundation to build our journey into hearing the voice of God. When the church embraces the truths in *Born to Hear God,* we shall see a supernatural church walking in love and power. I highly recommend this book to those hungry to grow in hearing the voice of God.

- Ivan Roman
Senior Leader of *Empowered Life Church*
Author of *Prophets Among Us*
Founder of *Friend of God Ministries*

I believe Dr. Luc Niebergall has given the body of Christ a beautiful gift in this book, *Born to Hear God*. One of the greatest revelations a person can come into after discovering that God loves them is that He also passionately desires to speak to them. The "Talking God" we encounter from Genesis 1 to Revelation 22 still talks today. While a significant portion of the body of Christ has awakened to the possibility of the current speaking of

God in the earth, prophecy, there still seems to be some misunderstanding—or immaturity—from a biblical perspective towards how we are to apply this reality to our everyday lives. In this book, Dr. Luc unpacks a relevant and biblically principled approach to understanding this precious aspect of our discipleship in Christ.

- David Balestri
National Convenor of the *Australian Coalition of Apostolic Leaders*
National Member of the *Australian Prophetic Council*

In *Born to Hear God,* Dr. Luc Niebergall shares essential principles to help develop a lifestyle of hearing God. Peppered with stories that build your faith, practical teaching, and helpful activations, you will find yourself on a tour of God's heart that leaves you longing for more of God. Luc brings clarity to various prophetic activities but keeps it anchored in relationship with God and love for people. His value for health in prophetic expression is crucial. I would highly recommend this book to anyone wanting to learn more about how God speaks.

- John E. Thomas
President of *Streams Ministries International*

Dr. Luc Niebergall's *Born to Hear God* is a prophetic-equipping masterpiece. In an era where the Body of Christ must hold to the biblical standard of pursuing the gifts of the Spirit, this book is the blueprint. God desires that all would hear and know His voice. Luc manages to unpack the mystery of "hearing God" while providing us with a profoundly user-friendly handbook to do just that.

- Derek Schneider
President of *History Makers Academy*
Founder of *History Makers Society*

Every person is created with a hard-wired capacity to recognize and respond to the voice of God. We are in an exciting season where God is raising prophetic voices to train, equip, and activate the gift of prophecy for all of His sons and daughters. More people are prophesying on the earth today than ever before, but we must not assume that the *operation* of the gift automatically means we are fully *trained* in it. Dr. Luc Niebergall's most recent book, *Born to Hear God,* is a refreshing and powerful tool that will equip the believer to grow in their understanding of what God's heart is for us as New Covenant believers and how it relates to prophetic ministry. This necessary resource teaches us how the prophetic can function the way God intended it to be: as a gift of love—and from Love Himself—to the world.

- Bethany Hicks
Author of *The God Connection* and *Own Your Assignment*
Co-founder of the *Prophetic Company*

Dr. Luc Niebergall takes readers on a journey into the vast world of the prophetic. *Born to Hear God* enlightens, illuminates, and re-aligns people to the multifaceted beauty of the voice of God.

- Chazdon Strickland
Founder of *Ignite the Globe*

Luc Niebergall's new book *Born to Hear God* is so necessary in today's season. Luc explains and empowers us that we can all hear God—not to just be *prophetic*—but to help transform other people's lives. I agree with Luc that God is looking for people who will pay the price to hear Him. Luc writes from his heart and shares so many real-life examples. This is a very informative and inspiring book.

- Alan Strudwick
Founder of *Alan Strudwick Ministries*
Kingdom Business Ministries
Author of Destiny Image's Book *Authentic Awakening*

The gift of prophecy is not an add-on to our faith, at least according to the New Testament. It is central to the new covenant we have received through Christ. Repeatedly, the New Testament requires the gift of prophecy as normative for the church, commanding us not to quench the Spirit nor despise prophecy. The author of Hebrews urges us, "Today, when you hear his voice (three times)," and conclusively adds, "Therefore, do not refuse the one who speaks!" We are created to hear the voice of our speaking God. In his book *Born to Hear God,* Dr. Luc Niebergall helps us step into our identity and purpose as a prophetic community that has received the prophetic Spirit, hears God's revelatory word, and gives prophetic charismatic witness to the world.

- **Rev. Dr. Kim Maas**
Kim Maas Ministries, Inc
Author of *Prophetic Community: God's Call for All to Minister in His Gifts* and *The Way of the Kingdom: Seizing the Times for a Great Move of God (Chosen Books)*

Born to Hear God

BORN TO HEAR GOD

AN IN-DEPTH LOOK AT THE PROPHETIC MINISTRY

DR. LUC NIEBERGALL

NOTE: If you purchased this book without a cover, you should be aware that this book is stolen property. It was reported as "unsold and destroyed" to the publisher, and neither the author nor the publisher has received payment for this "stripped book." No part of this publication may be reproduced, stored in a retrieval system, or transmitted, in any form or by any means, electronic, mechanical, photocopying, recording or otherwise, without prior written permission from the author or publisher.

Unless otherwise noted, all Scripture references in this book are taken from the New King James Version®, copyright © 1982 by Thomas Nelson. Used by permission. All rights reserved.

BORN TO HEAR GOD

Copyright © 2024 by Luc Niebergall

Copy Editor: Sarah Reimer

Cover Design: Todd Toews

ISBN: 9798342670289

All rights reserved.

Printed in Canada

DEDICATION

I dedicate this book to my sweetheart, Sophie Niebergall. Sophie, as I've travelled the world teaching the principles written throughout this book, you've been by my side the whole time. You've provided endless support, prayer, and affirmation, empowering me to live out my God-given destiny. Thank you for championing me. I couldn't do what I do without you by my side.

Contents

Foreword by *Patricia King* – 15

Foreword by *Lana Vawser* - 21

Chapter 1: The Heart of the Prophetic - 29

Chapter 2: Beginning to Hear - 49

Chapter 3: Speaking Forth - 71

Chapter 4: Vision - 85

Chapter 5: Prophecy - 103

Chapter 6: Words of Knowledge - 119

Chapter 7: Messages of Wisdom - 133

Chapter 8: Discerning of Spirits - 147

Chapter 9: Prophetic Pitfalls - 165

Chapter 10: Prophetic Community - 181

Chapter 11: Prophetic Leadership - 191

Chapter 12: Prophetic Mandate - 205

Foreword
Patricia King

There is a longing in the heart of every believer—a deep desire to hear the voice of God and experience His tangible presence. It's a yearning that transcends culture, age, and background because it is woven into the very fabric of who we are as His creation. When God formed man from the dust of the earth and breathed His Spirit into him, He breathed life, purpose, and, most importantly, connection. This connection is not one-sided. God did not design us merely to know about Him, but to *know* Him, to walk with Him in a dynamic, living relationship. And central to that relationship is communication—hearing His voice.

Dr. Luc Niebergall's book, *Born to Hear God*, is not just another message about hearing the voice of the Lord. It is divinely inspired for such a time as this, urging the Church to return to the simplicity and beauty of communion with our Creator. This book addresses a truth that has been too often neglected or misunderstood: that we, as believers, are not only capable of hearing God but we were *designed* to hear Him.

One of the greatest deceptions that the enemy has propagated within the Body of Christ is that hearing God's voice is for a select few—the prophets, the pastors, the spiritual "elite." Many believers have been led to believe that God is distant, silent, or disinterested in their lives. They may see Him as a distant figure, only speaking through His Word or through others, but not directly to them. This lie has left many Christians disillusioned, believing they are unworthy or incapable of discerning the voice of the Lord for themselves.

But here's the truth: *Every believer has been born to hear God.*

The Scriptures are full of accounts where God spoke directly to His people. From Adam and Eve in the garden to Moses at the burning bush, to the prophets, and ultimately through Jesus Christ—God has always sought a relationship that includes intimate communication. Jesus Himself declared in John 10:27, "My sheep hear My voice, and I know them, and they follow Me." This statement is clear: those who belong to Him hear His voice. It's not a matter of *if* you can hear God, but rather *how* you recognize and respond to His voice.

Luc, in *Born to Hear God*, masterfully navigates this profound subject by breaking down the barriers that have hindered so many from experiencing God's voice in their daily lives. With a teacher's heart and the wisdom of someone who has walked this journey intimately with the Lord, Luc unveils powerful biblical truths that awaken the reader to their divine identity as a son or daughter who has been given access to the very heart of God.

One of the things I appreciate most about this book is Luc's ability to make hearing God accessible to everyone. Whether you are a seasoned believer or someone new to the faith, *Born to Hear God* provides both the theological foundation and practical steps necessary to cultivate a lifestyle of listening to the Lord. Luc doesn't just tell us that we *can* hear God; he shows us *how* to develop the ears to listen. Through clear teaching and practical exercises, he helps readers identify the ways God is already speaking to them—whether through Scripture, the inner witness of the Holy Spirit, dreams, visions, or through the beauty of creation around us.

In a world that is increasingly filled with noise and distractions, it is more important than ever to cultivate a discerning ear that is tuned to the frequency of heaven. We live in a time where many voices compete for our attention—voices of fear, doubt, discouragement, and confusion. But amid the clamour, God's voice is still and steady, a whisper of peace, love, and direction. As Luc points out, hearing God is not about striving; it's about quieting ourselves, aligning our hearts with His, and trusting that He *is* speaking.

Another critical aspect that Luc addresses is the issue of trust. Many believers struggle to trust that what they are hearing is indeed from God. They doubt their ability to hear accurately or worry that they might be deceived. Luc tackles this head-on, teaching us how to distinguish God's voice from other influences, and how to discern with confidence what He is saying. He brings clarity to the process of hearing God, which in turn builds faith and removes the fear of getting it wrong.

Furthermore, Luc's writing is saturated with testimonies of how hearing God has transformed lives.

Each story serves as a powerful reminder that God is not distant or silent—He is near, and He is speaking. These testimonies not only inspire faith but stir a deep hunger within the reader to press in and cultivate their own relationship with the Lord. As you read, you'll find yourself being drawn into a deeper place of intimacy with God, where His voice becomes the guiding light for every step you take.

I believe that *Born to Hear God* is a book that will awaken the Body of Christ to the fullness of what it means to live in relationship with the God who speaks. It is an invitation to every believer to step into the reality of hearing God for themselves—not as a once-in-a-while occurrence, but as a daily, vibrant experience. Luc has provided a roadmap for anyone who desires to know the voice of their Shepherd more intimately, and I am confident that those who embrace the truths within these pages will experience a profound shift in their spiritual walk.

In closing, I want to encourage you as you begin reading *Born to Hear God*. Open your heart wide, because God is ready to speak to you in ways you've never imagined. The Father is inviting you to lean in, to listen, and to trust that His voice is accessible to you. You are *not* disqualified, and you are certainly not forgotten. You were created with ears to hear Him.

God has deep and profound intel to share with you— His thoughts, His heart, His plans. He desires to speak into every area of your life, whether it's in the small, everyday decisions or the significant moments of destiny. You have been given the incredible privilege to hear the voice of the Creator of the universe.

As you read this book, my prayer is that you will step into a new level of intimacy with God and that your ears will be opened to the sound of His voice in ways that are fresh, exciting, and life-changing.

You were born to hear God. Embrace this truth and allow it to transform every aspect of your life.

- Patricia King
Patricia King Ministries

Foreword
Lana Vawser

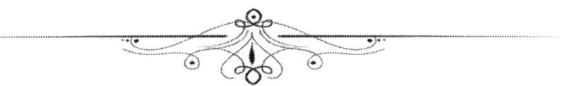

As believers, we are invited into this deep and beautiful place of intimacy with Jesus. It's a place of living so close to His heart, nestled deeply in the secret place of communion with Him to know Him, to hear His voice, and to make Him known.

I remember being a sixteen-year-old girl coming to know Jesus and instantly experiencing a supernatural hunger to hear from God. I would have climbed the highest mountain and gone to the ends of the earth to hear His voice. I was so profoundly and supernaturally awakened to love and the reality of intimacy with Jesus, and the invitation to know the Father and His heart and to hear His voice. I remember being so marked by the truth of John 10:27:

"My sheep hear My voice, and I know them, and they follow Me."

I was completely overtaken, consumed, and filled with a hunger to hear His voice. The God of the universe, almighty God, the Creator of the heavens, the majestic One, the one and only true living God, wants to have a relationship with me and invites me to hear His voice daily. That revelation, among others in that season, changed my life forever. I committed my life in that season to be one who was radically abandoned to Christ, to know Him, to position myself to hear His voice, and to live daily in the reality of the invitation of Matthew 4:4:

"Man shall not live by bread alone but by every word that proceeds from the mouth of God."

Not only was I distinctly marked in that season—that for all my days I wanted to live IN and FROM His voice in every area of my life—I wanted to steward His voice well with integrity, purity, and humility, and to carry His heart contained WITHIN His voice, well. It has been my passion for decades now to live completely yielded and surrendered to Him and the leading of His voice. It has been my passion to champion and raise up others to live from that place of deep intimacy and friendship with God and to see their partnership with His Spirit and His voice to see His Kingdom extended and lives transformed. The depth of revelation of WHO it is that speaks to us, WHOSE voice we hear, has forever changed my life and continues to burn deeply within me every day.

In reading through the pages of this incredible gift that the Lord has given you—through His friend Dr. Luc Niebergall—my heart was filled with such excitement. I was filled with anticipation, knowing that the Lord has set a table for you, a feast of His wisdom, revelation, and insight that will position you firmly in the revelation that you were BORN TO HEAR GOD. It is your design.

Throughout these pages, Dr. Luc shares weighty wisdom, revelation, and practical stories that will equip you on your journey of hearing from God and moving in the prophetic. Luc places incredible value on stewarding the voice of the Lord WELL and carrying His heart with sensitivity, purity, integrity, and wisdom. The pages are dripping with intimacy. I could feel the depths of Luc's friendship with the Lord and his passion for you to flourish in your journey exploring the prophetic realms that are before you.

Can I encourage you as you read these pages? Read them slowly. Allow the Holy Spirit to minister deeply to you. Take your time going through the chapters and the activations as I see the fire of God falling upon you to fuel that first-love fire within you. The Lord desires that you encounter the fire of His presence and His voice on another level through this beautiful gift the Holy Spirit has given to you through Luc.

Thank you, Dr. Luc, for your yielded yes to the Lord. Thank you for partnering with Him to bring forth such a gift to the body of Christ as we all continue to grow together in hearing His voice, carrying His heart, and stewarding His revelation and the prophetic with purity, integrity, humility, maturity, and sensitivity.

- **Lana Vawser**
Prophetic Voice and Author

PART I
Prophetic Foundations

Prophecy is a heavenly tool empowering us to pierce hearts with the Father's love.

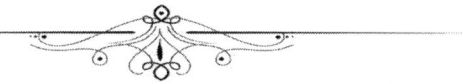

CHAPTER ONE
The Heart of the Prophetic

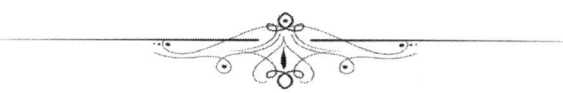

You were born to hear God.

Yes, you read that right. You weren't *born* by random happening—your life is one of far greater importance. You were designed for purpose, born for friendship with the very one who imagined you into being. You were shaped to walk so closely with Him that you hear His faintest of whispers, called to come so near that you will be entrusted with the deep secrets of His heart. My friend, you are a child of significance and you were fashioned for connection with the very heart of God.

The prophetic ministry—being attuned to the voice of God—burns deeply within me. When I was much younger, I received a call from the Lord as a prophetic voice to the church. For almost two decades, I've had the great honour of travelling throughout Canada and to different nations, training God's people how to hear Him. I can't think of many things more exciting than witnessing people experiencing the voice of God for the first time. As they hear Him, it's almost as though you can tangibly see them adopting a newfound revelation of identity. In the very moment of hearing, they understand that they aren't weary wanderers who must fumble through life. They are sons and daughters who get to be guided by the voice of the Father, the Son, and Holy Spirit. I've seen the voice of God heal the most broken of hearts. I've watched His word align the most impossible circumstances.

Just as I've witnessed the voice of God transform hearts time and time again, He wants to do the very same for you. It doesn't matter what nation you live in. It doesn't matter whether you are currently sitting in a coffee shop or lounging in your bed. It doesn't matter what process you face or how broken your past is. The Father wants to speak affirming words to you. Jesus wants to talk with you as a friend speaks to a friend. Holy Spirit wants to reveal divine secrets to you.

God wants to encounter you with His voice.

The Father's Pursuit

I fondly remember the first time I saw a tangible breakthrough through a prophetic word I'd spoken. I was eighteen, sitting in a coffee shop with a warm drink in my hand. Suddenly, my attention shifted to a man sitting a few tables down from mine. He was a middle-aged man who was writing in his journal. I could feel the heart of God for him, compassion flooding my heart.

Immediately, in my mind, I saw a vision.

The vision was nothing dramatic, seeming like little more than a fleeting thought. I saw this man as a small child running through a field, trying to catch a butterfly. No matter how hard he tried, the butterfly was always just beyond his hand's grasp. I then heard the words subtly run through my mind, *"I'm about to open doors for this man that he has been praying would open, and I'm about to close doors that he has been praying to close."*

Trying my best to force my nerves to subside, I slowly rose from my seat. As I approached the man, I didn't know that both of our lives were about to be transformed.

After nervously introducing myself, I said, "I believe God speaks today, and I feel like I received a message for you. Do you mind if I share with you what I felt like the Lord said?"

The man nodded his approval, inviting me to continue.

The memory of the vision still playing through my mind, I said, "I felt that God said that ever since you were a child, you have felt like you've been chasing beauty, yet it has been just out of hand's grasp. I feel He is saying that He is about to open doors in your life that you have been praying would open, and He is closing doors that you have prayed would close."

The man stared at me with bewildered eyes. He slid his journal across the table and said, "Right before you walked up to my table, I was writing in this journal. Read what I just wrote."

The journal entry read:

"Dear God, ever since I was a child, I have felt like I've been chasing beauty, yet it has been just out of hand's grasp. Open the doors that I have prayed would open and close the doors that I have

prayed would close."

As I read the honest words, chills raced over my body. In truth, what marked me more than what the man wrote were his eyes. Budding with tears, they looked both in awe and—at the same time—undone. It was the look of someone whose heart had transformed in a split moment. It was the look of one who had encountered the Father heart of God.

As a young man, that one encounter showed me that someone's life could be transformed by the word of God. I definitively knew that God hadn't lost His voice. He still speaks, and He's longing for His children to *hear*. It was at this moment that I learned that the purpose of the prophetic ministry is to connect people to the heart of the Father. This is why the prophetic ministry cannot be cast aside. In fact, it's worth adamantly pursuing.

1 Corinthians 14:1: "Pursue love, and desire spiritual gifts, but especially that you may prophesy."

The word *desire* is a powerful one. Though it's not enough to merely desire—we need to understand *why* we should. Something you'll learn about me is that I'm an avid believer in heart health. I believe that weighty gifts are to be wielded by healthy hearts. That said, we shouldn't desire to prophesy to appease our own insecurities. God doesn't gift us for our sakes, but because He loves those around us. He gifts us so we can bridge the heart of the Father to others.

Quite some time ago, I was ministering at a conference that spanned throughout a weekend. On the Friday night, I spoke and ministered. God was moving wonderfully, pouring out in prophecy and healing. At the end of the service, person after person came up to me for prayer.

One woman, around thirty years old, approached me. One thing differed her from the others who came for prayer; she had a worn and old teddy bear tucked underneath her arm. Assuming she must have had a child with her, I didn't give it more thought.

As I began to pray over her, I could hear Holy Spirit whispering to me that He wanted to release freedom and peace over her. I prayed out loud, saying, "God is releasing freedom over you right now. He is establishing peace in your life where there wasn't peace before."

She quietly cried for a time and then dismissed herself. I didn't think more about this interaction until I saw her at the church the following day. This woman approached me; however, there was something different about her: she wasn't carrying the teddy bear.

She said to me, "I need to tell you something. You probably noticed I had a teddy bear with me last night, didn't you?"

I nodded my head, inviting her to continue.

She said, "I was severely abused as a child. Because of what I went through, I found comfort in my teddy bear. I brought it everywhere with me—it became my safe place. Due to what I went through, I've developed several anxiety disorders. As an adult, I've carried my childhood teddy bear everywhere with me. Any time I would go anywhere, I would bring it with me. If I didn't, I would have a panic attack. When you spoke those words over me last night, I felt anxiety leaving me."

With tears streaming down her face, she then held out her hands, saying, "This is the first time since being a child when I've gone somewhere without my teddy bear and I haven't had a panic attack. Jesus has set me free from anxiety disorders. I now know that He is my *safe place*."

Time and time again, I've watched God use the prophetic ministry as a tool to heal broken hearts, free people from mental health disorders, restore families, and guide people to salvation. There is an age-old teaching that says: Seek the Giver and *not* the gifts. While I can appreciate the heart behind such a proverb, it's not entirely accurate. We certainly need to seek the *Giver*—first and foremost. If you've sat through any of my teachings, you've heard me share about friendship with God. It's the topic that burns deepest in my heart. However, the truth is that there is a broken world around us. People are crying out for an encounter with the heart of God. Prophecy is a heavenly tool, empowering us to pierce hearts with the Father's love.

Isaiah 50:4: "The Lord God has given Me the tongue of the learned, that I should know how to speak a word in season to him who is weary. He awakens Me morning by morning, He awakens My ear to hear as the learned."

<u>History of the Prophetic</u>

Several years ago, I was driving in my car through country roads, communing with the Lord. As my eyes scoured over hilly landscapes of Alberta, Canada, I felt the presence of God come upon me. It felt as though a *healing anointing* entered my car. Considering my wife and I have seen many types of healings throughout the span of our ministry, I have a significant value for the Lord showing up in such a way.

I asked the Lord, "What type of healing anointing is this that you're placing on my life? Is it for physical healing? Inner healing? Healing of the mind?"

Immediately, Holy Spirit spoke to me, saying, "This anointing is for bringing healing to people's doctrines."

While I'm primarily graced as a prophetic leader, secondarily, God has gifted me to teach. Due to my giftset and personality, in many ways, I'm both a mystic and an intellectual. My heart burns to take truths perceived as complicated and simplify them to be made palatable for many. I have a deep love for the supernatural things of God; I also have a deep love for such things to be articulated and taught well. The prophetic ministry is one that I believe has been direly overlooked, greatly misunderstood, and—at times—unnecessarily mystified. My heart is to simplify it, to help reveal to you your access to God's voice.

We are living in a time when God is healing our doctrine concerning the prophetic ministry. Depending on where I minister, the comfort level around hearing God varies. Sometimes when I teach on the prophetic, I'm met with excitement, and other times, I'm met with anxious stares. Unfortunately, to say that the prophetic ministry has always been utilized properly wouldn't be a truthful statement. There have been many demonstrations of health, as well as times when it wasn't modelled with wisdom and care. I want to take time to unpack for you the recent history of the prophetic ministry.

Throughout the last century, we've seen various moves of God that have swept throughout the earth. We experienced the *Azusa Street Revival* in 1906, where we caught a revelation of revival. We saw mass salvations during the *Jesus People Movement* in the 1960s and 1970s. There have been various moves where fresh revelation infused into the church. It was in the 1980s when a wave of the prophetic swept throughout the church on a grand scale. Before this, the church lived through a drought of not hearing the voice of God for decades. God was no doubt *speaking*, but the church wasn't equipped to *hear*. In the 1980s, for the first time in decades, it wasn't only the few who heard God; the masses did. Visions increased. People received the word of the Lord through dreams. Church meetings would erupt as prophetic utterances spilled forth. Lives were radically marked and changed by the spoken word of God.

I've been a student of church history for quite some time. Historically, whenever God pours out a new revelation to the masses, a pivotal time of adjustment takes place. It's not enough to simply catch a new revelation; we need to receive it with wisdom and maturity. If we don't, we risk pulling the pendulum from one extreme to the other, instead of finding the healthy medium.

In this instance, if the former side of the pendulum was not hearing God at all, the opposite—the latter side—would be hearing Him but not having the proper teachings, protocol, and parameters. While in many prophetic circles, health was fostered with this outpouring, in others, it wasn't. We saw a demonstration of both health and dysfunction in the prophetic ministry. Many no doubt benefitted from hearing the spoken word of God; however, due to a lack of teaching and an inexperience with this particular ministry, we also saw it misused. While many were uplifted, many were also hurt.

It's easy to look back and see that the gift had, at times, been misused, although it's imperative to understand the *why*. Here is what I believe happened:

When the church caught a revelation of the prophetic ministry in the 1980s, we examined the New Testament, looking for an embodiment of a prophetic leader. It didn't take long for many emerging prophetic communities to discover that there is not a vast amount of New Testament prophets written about in Scripture for us to study. In fact, the variety of those who were actually called *prophets*—other than Jesus—is minimal, leaving us with only Agabus (Acts 21:10), Judas, and Silas (Acts 15:32). For all three of these men, there is very little mentioning. Since we didn't see an embodiment of a prophetic figure, we, unfortunately, dismissed Paul's teachings and protocols in 1 Corinthians 14 concerning the prophetic ministry. Since we didn't see many prophets to refer to in the New Testament, the body of Christ looked where there was a vast variety of prophets: the Old Testament.

The church began to use the Old Testament prophets as a template of how to prophesy. Unintentionally, as New Testament people, we stepped into an Old Covenant mindset and began to prophesy under Old Testament principles.

Here's how Old Testament prophecy worked: since in the Old Testament Jesus hadn't yet died on the cross, sin still stood as a barrier between man and God. A prophet's function was to point out the sin that was rampant in individuals, cities, and nations in the hope that the people would repent. If they did indeed repent and turn from their sin, then there would be a form of *right standing* established between man and God. If the people didn't repent, the prophet would then pronounce the repercussions of their sins. Since it was a completely different covenant than what we currently live under, Old Testament prophecy functioned as one to expose for the purpose of repentance. If repentance wasn't offered, then judgement was pronounced.

Imagine if we pulled this way of ministry into New Testament times. Imagine if we used prophetic gifts to expose every hint of dirt we could find and to pronounce judgement. To say we would find ourselves in a mess would be a dire understatement. Ever since this point in history, many in the church have been in a process of healing due to these misconceptions concerning prophecy.

Paul laid out an excellent protocol for New Testament prophecy:

1 Corinthians 14:3: "He who prophesies speaks edification and exhortation and comfort to men."

While Old Testament prophecy brought judgement, New Testament prophecy brings *edification* (which means "improvement"), *exhortation* (which means "encouragement"), and comfort. That isn't to say there aren't times of correction, warning, or direction—I'll cover this in a later chapter. However, we need to understand that the expression of prophecy has shifted because the covenant we live under has changed.

Elijah was a profound prophet. He accomplished unfathomable feats throughout his ministry. His ministry consisted of slaying the four hundred false prophets and calling down fire from heaven to consume his foes (1 Kings 18 and 2 Kings 1). We could rejoice in this because it was a completely different covenant.

Take a look at this:

Malachi 4:5-6: "Behold, I will send Elijah the prophet before the coming of the great and dreadful day of the Lord. And he will turn the hearts of the fathers to the children, and the hearts of the children to their fathers."

There is a fascinating detail for us to grasp in these verses. Elijah's prophetic ministry in the Old Testament consisted of slaying false prophets; in the New Testament, it's about reconciling families. Elijah's ministerial expression concerning prophecy totally changed because the covenant man lived under shifted.

For over a decade, I ministered in a specific city. When I first began, I started putting on classes, training people to hear the voice of God. I was surprised to see how reluctant and offended people were towards the prophetic ministry. They were terrified of it. I began poking around, asking pastors and leaders in the city why people had such a strong reaction to any teaching regarding prophecy.

I found out that fifteen years prior to my ministering in the city, another prophetic leader had done a lot of ministry in the area. This man heard God in specific detail. I was dumbfounded by the stories of how profound his gift was. There was, however, a very public fall that took place with him concerning a sexual scandal, resulting in prison time. He also used his gift as a tool of judgement rather than as one of reconciliation to the Father. It was very overt and disastrous for the city. This scandal disbursed a wound throughout the people he had influenced.

Upon realizing this, the Lord spoke to me, saying, "Help Me restore what has been broken. Build in this city."

"For how long?" I asked.

He didn't hesitate to reply, saying, "Seeing Me bring restoration to the prophetic ministry in this city is going to cost a decade of your life."

As a prophetic minister, I no doubt had my work cut out. With my wife, Sophie, by my side, we plowed what felt at times to be impossible ground. We continued putting on small classes, schools, and seminars. Over the years, we saw minor fluctuations of growth; however, in all honesty, it was difficult. Ten years into our building and training in the city, we put on an event. We said that whoever attended would get their own personal prophetic word from those I had trained in our team. We expected anywhere from about fifty to eighty people to show up. To our surprise, almost five hundred people came!

I remember looking over that crowd, seeing the hunger for the spoken word of God that I had never seen before in this city. People came up to us weeping, saying, "We remember when you only had ten people coming to learn about hearing the voice of God. Now look at this!"

My wife and I sowed over a decade of our lives into that city. We planted our first ministry school there. We trained leaders, speakers, and authors. In many ways, I watched God restore a city. I learned how influence in the prophetic can bring both wounding *and* healing on a large scale, depending on how it is represented. This instilled within me a deep fear of the Lord. It taught me how serious it is for us as leaders to guard our hearts with all diligence. It taught me how God longs for the prophetic ministry to be healthy.

While many have been hurt by misuse of the prophetic, we must remember to never disregard something so precious to God's heart. People yearning to hear God's voice has nothing to do with glorifying the prophetic ministry; it has everything to do with glorifying *Jesus the Prophet*. He deserves His rightful place in the body of Christ. He deserves to be represented well.

Eyes to See

If I were to simplify what prophecy is in New Testament times, it is to tap into the voice of God, speaking His very word and heart into people, families, communities, cities, and nations. The prophetic ministry is a tool to communicate God's word into people's callings, relationships, finances, seasons of life, and much more. A predominant part of the prophetic ministry is to look at people through the eyes of heaven—through the eyes of the Father—and to speak that forth. Prophecy reveals kingdom identity. It calls forth calling and destiny.

I have always found Samson from Judges 13-16 an intriguing person in the Bible. Samson was the strongest man recorded in Scripture, yet his size or physique was never mentioned. On the other hand, Goliath's appearance was described in great detail (1 Samuel 17:4-7). Considering that Samson had a greater reputation concerning strength, one would assume that something about his size would have been mentioned. I believe the reason his size wasn't mentioned is that Samson was likely a regular man in size. The truth is that God hides greatness in human vessels. As prophetic people, our job is to see through one another's humanity and normality to see the essence of Christ's divinity hidden within.

1 Samuel 16:7: "'The LORD said to Samuel, 'Do not look at his appearance or at his physical stature, because I have refused him. For the LORD does not see as man sees; for man looks at the outward appearance, but the LORD looks at the heart.'"

What would it look like to see people as God sees them?

Something I consider to be a great privilege in my life is that I have the honour of speaking prophetically into the ears of the influential. I get to prophesy the word of the Lord into the lives of respected government leaders, CEOs, church leaders, and celebrities in the arts and entertainment industry. There are times when I meet many of these leaders through *divine appointments*. Other times, having heard of my prophetic ministry, they seek me out. Most often, I will meet them before their names are known. I get to discern their potential, seeing them in a way that only God sees them.

Years ago, a young man I didn't know at the time reached out to me, asking to meet for a coffee. Unfortunately, due to my strict traveling and writing schedule, I can't do as many meetings like this as I would like. Nonetheless, I felt the Lord prompting me, saying, "Make sure you prioritize this meeting."

I met with this young man and heard his story. He shared about how he was navigating through direction for his life. We had a great time getting to know one another when God spoke to me.

He said, "Make this young man a priority. He's a rising celebrity and is called to have mass influence in the music industry."

I looked at him, all of a sudden perceiving him as more than a twenty-three-year-old young adult fumbling his way through life. I saw him the way that God saw him. I saw his potential. At that moment, I had the honour of speaking to him about his calling and destiny.

I watched him throughout the next five years as he pursued a music career. Profound doors began opening for him. It didn't take long before he was in the top ten charts in all of North America in his particular genre of music. Throughout his journey in rising to fame, he diligently pursued the Lord and has had significant impact on many lives through his life and music. He's remained a friend to this day.

This is the power of the prophetic ministry. The word of the Lord can put things into motion that wouldn't be otherwise. It can be a catalyst for the remarkable. As prophetic people, we have the ability to see others the way God sees them. When we look at people through natural understanding, we see them through a temporal lens. We see their physical appearance, circumstances, past, and current season of life. When we look at people through supernatural understanding, we see something rather different. We see them through eternity's perspective. We can see the gold of their potential and speak that forth.

All around us, there are people who don't know who they are. Their true identity is buried beneath false labels, lies, and pain. The Father has given you eyes to look deeper, to see who He has truly created them to be.

Child of God, through the cross you have been given a precious gift: to know the Father. You can hear His faintest of whispers. You can feel His heartbeat.

You can see the way He sees.

Dr. Luc Niebergall

Prayer

Pray this with me:

"God, I thank You that You still speak today. I thank You that You speak to me. I pray for ears to hear and eyes to see. Jesus, I receive You in my life as my Prophet. I release to You any misconceptions, offences, or hurts concerning how You speak. Create in me a deep hunger to hear You. Give me a heart for those around me that I may speak Your word, bridging people to encounter the Father.

"*Amen.*"

Prophetic Activation

The purpose of prophetic activations is to provide a safe and guided experience while learning to hear God.

In this activation, I want you to ask God a simple question. Depending on the person, this exercise will be most effective either through verbally speaking or through journaling. Feel free to do whichever you feel will help you best.

As you ask, still your mind and wait on Him. Remember that God might speak to you through the still, internal voice. He may speak to you through impressions or pictures in your mind.

Question: "God, what do you love about me?"

Once you feel like you receive an answer, write down what He said.

*Friendship with God requires communication.
It requires listening.*

Chapter Two
Beginning to Hear

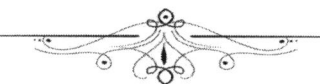

In this very moment—in your current situation and season of life—God is speaking to you. His voice is real, showering over you to give clarity, affirmation, and direction.

This poses the question: If God is speaking, why do we struggle to hear?

This is a profound question. It's one that I suppose most have wrestled with at one time or another in their lifetime. The first principle we need to know is that hearing Him starts from the place of *friendship*.

When people look at my current life, they see me travelling and speaking. They see me fathering voices and speaking prophetically into lives. I'm not ashamed to say that this isn't where my story began in hearing God's voice. It didn't start on a mountaintop but in the valley.

My journey in hearing God's voice began when Holy Spirit spoke to me right after I was marked and saved at the ripe age of sixteen, saying, "Luc, you are called to ministry; however, your calling is not conventional. Since your calling isn't conventional, neither will your training be. Many called to go into ministry are called to four years of Bible college. For you, your training will be lying on your face before Me for four years."

My training to hear the voice of God began on my face; it began in friendship. These four years were precious ones in my life. I didn't have a stage to speak from. I wasn't recognized as a "prophetic leader." All I had was Him. I had an adamant hunger to know God and to hear His voice. I remember in this season, for hours on end, walking with Him with a notebook in hand. I would walk, pray, and practice hearing Him. It was in this place where specific verses came alive to me—became a part of me.

John 10:27: "My sheep hear My voice, and I know them, and they follow Me."

Friendship with God is no doubt my absolute favourite topic. It is the foundation for everything I do in life. Friendship with Him should encompass the entirety of our lives. Since I've written in great detail about this in previous works, I will leave the teaching at a minimum in this book. I would highly encourage you to read my book *Pioneer*. It is saturated with teaching and revelation on friendship with God; it's perhaps the most important thing I've written to date.

I will, however, say this: if we refuse God in friendship, then all we are left with is religion. This doesn't only apply to things such as *religious doings*; it also applies to the supernatural things of God.

This fundamental truth reminds me of Jesus' now-famous quote, "Not everyone who says to Me, 'Lord,

Lord,' shall enter the kingdom of heaven, but He who does the will of My Father in heaven. Many will say to Me in that day, 'Lord, Lord, have we not prophesied in Your name, cast out demons in Your name, and done many wonders in Your name?' And then I will declare to them, 'I never knew you; depart from Me, you who practice lawlessness!'" (Matthew 7:21-23).

What a sobering set of verses. Many have tried to use them to discredit prophecy; however, this isn't the context of these verses. Instead, they discredit prophecy apart from *knowing Him*. We need to seek and function in the gifts from the place of friendship, or we risk operating in power from impure motives, religious mentalities, and striving, rather than being moved by encounter.

The prophetic ministry, when it's done right, isn't *only* about walking in spiritual giftedness; it is about communing with the heart of God. It's about building closeness to the heart of Jesus to the point where He will reveal His secrets to us. This is why friendship needs to be the foundation of the prophetic. In many ways, I could say that *basic prophetic* says, "I want a prophetic word." Whereas *mature prophetic* says, "I want to know the secrets of God's heart." Being entrusted with secrets requires unwavering closeness.

There is a distinct contrast between someone who prophesies from gifting and someone who does so from friendship. Numbers 22 shares a story about a man named Balaam. There is no doubt that Balaam had a weighty prophetic gift. He could give accurate prophetic words, predicting the future. He could bless something and it would thrive; he could curse something and it would diminish. Balaam, however, didn't walk in this level of accuracy because of his closeness to God; it was simply his gift in fruition.

There is a clear difference between Balaam and someone like Abraham, who was called a friend of God (Isaiah 41:8). Genesis 18 shares a profound story. We read that God was going to destroy Sodom and Gomorrah due to their sin and corruption. Right before God acts, He asks Himself a profound question. I believe it to be one of the most intimate questions in the Bible.

God says, "Shall I hide from Abraham what I am doing?" (Genesis 18:17).

This is remarkable to me. In this scenario, God is about to move and act. Instead, He thinks of Abraham and chooses to share what is in His heart. God walked so intimately with Abraham that He wanted to invite this man into His process. God felt as though He would be betraying His friendship with Abraham if He didn't share the secrets of His heart.

In his gifting, Balaam could prophesy accurate words. He could predict the future; however, he differed greatly from Abraham. Balaam prophesied from gifting; Abraham heard God from friendship. Friends are the ones who are entrusted with the deep secrets of God's heart. They receive an ear to hear what burns in the heart of God.

Amos 3:7: "Surely the Lord God does nothing, unless He reveals His secret to His servants the prophets."

God has no obligation to share His secrets with prophets. He is under no contract to do so. He shares His secrets with the prophets because they are His friends. This should be the goal of the prophetic ministry: getting so close to the Lord in friendship that if He is going to act and move, He can't help but share with us first.

The Language of God

Friendship with God requires communication. It requires listening. Mastering communication requires understanding *language*.

When Jesus was tempted by Satan in the wilderness, He said something fascinating: "Man shall not live by bread alone, but by every word of God" (Luke 4:4). In the Greek language, there are two terms for *word*. There is the *logos* word, which means "written word"—this is referring to Scripture. There is also the *rhema* word, which refers to "spoken word"—this is the prophetic word. In this verse when Jesus says that man lives by every word of God, the vocabulary that Jesus uses here is the *rhema* word. Man shall not live by bread alone but by the *spoken* word of God. Jesus is saying that we get our sustenance from God speaking to us. If Jesus Himself saying this doesn't propel us into wanting to understand how God speaks, then I'm convinced nothing will.

Even those we would consider to be seasoned in hearing the voice of God had to first become students. Samuel was no doubt a profound man of God. In 1 Samuel 3, we get to see a glimpse of him in his pre-prophet years. As a child, Samuel was lying by the ark of God. The Lord called his name audibly. When Samuel heard his name being called, he mistook it for his mentor Eli's voice. Samuel arose and said to Eli, "Here I am, for you called me" (1 Samuel 3:5).

Eli told Samuel that he didn't call his name and instructed him to lie back down. When Samuel lay down, the Lord called him again by name. Samuel again went to Eli, only to receive the same response.

God called Samuel a third time, except this time when Samuel went to Eli, the priest realized that this was God speaking. Eli said to Samuel, "Go, lie down; and it shall be, if He calls you, that you must say, 'Speak, Lord, for Your servant hears'" (1 Samuel 3:9).

The fourth time Samuel lay down, God called to Samuel and he responded, "Speak, for Your servant hears" (v. 10).

Samuel, in his younger years, was experiencing an audible-voice encounter with the Lord. However, since he didn't understand how God spoke, he didn't even know that it was Him. Samuel and God had a communication disconnect, primarily because Samuel didn't recognize His voice.

This is where many of us struggle. We believe God can speak, but we struggle with hearing because we don't know how to identify His language.

I often compare hearing God to when we first get married. If you are married, you will likely understand the analogy well:

Sophie and I met and married in our early twenties. The first time I talked with her, I was convinced that moment that I had met my best friend. When we were first married, we began a journey of learning the art of *communication*. Communication is a fascinating thing when you're learning to get to know someone more deeply. You can say one thing, yet it's heard in a completely other way. This is why newlyweds get into silly arguments about, say, what to eat for dinner or where to go on vacation. It's usually not someone intentionally being difficult, more often it's a matter of communication or lack thereof. Sophie and I, in the beginning, navigated learning communication, and now that years have passed, I can confidently say our communication has solidified. I am able to simply look at her, and based on her facial expression or body language, I know what she's thinking. She can do the same with me. This is the fruit of genuinely and intimately knowing someone. It is this very thing that we can cultivate with the Lord.

From here, I am going to highlight a few foundational ways that God speaks to us.

The Written Word of God

Let's start with one of the more obvious and practical ways that God can speak to us. First and foremost, we know that He speaks through His written Word.

Hebrews 4:12: "For the word of God is living and powerful, and sharper than any two-edged sword, piercing even to the division of soul and spirit, and of joints and marrow, and is a discerner of the thoughts and intents of the heart."

In the previous section, I gave a scriptural example for the *rhema* word of God, whereas this verse gives us an example of the *logos* word. God's Word is living and active.

When I was newly saved, I was so hungry to encounter God through the Bible. This appetite was amplified when He spoke to me, saying, "I can only entrust you with My spoken prophetic revelation for the church to the extent that you root yourself in My written Word."

I took this statement seriously, though I had a distinct obstacle distancing me from my heart's desire: I was dyslexic. I would spend countless hours trying to read

God's Word; the words and sentences formed a jumbled mess in my mind. While I could make out verses after much time and stress, I could feel frustration swelling in my heart. As a young believer, I was moved by passion, doing what I could only think to do. For almost a year, every night, I would place my Bible under my pillow as an act of faith. I would literally sleep all night with my head resting upon the Word.

While falling asleep, I would plead, saying, "God, I need Your Word in me."

It was a few short years later when God healed me from dyslexia, as well as from a plethora of other learning disabilities. He healed me while I wrote my first book.

Looking back at this almost twenty years later, I see that God hadn't only healed me from dyslexia so that I could read; He has used me to teach His Word all across Canada and in different parts of the world. I'm so thankful that God doesn't look for those who are perfect. He looks for a hunger to know Him.

The Bible isn't a dead word. It is alive because it is God-breathed. Every word and verse in the Bible is an open door for us to come into a revelatory encounter with Jesus. As Holy Spirit teaches us through His written Word, the *logos* word becomes *rhema* to us. I personally can't count how many times I've been faced with a decision and Holy Spirit whispers a verse to me, bringing direction. Or, I'll pick up my Bible, and a key story gives me clarity on how to move forward.

To everyone I train to hear God's voice, I stress the importance of being deeply rooted in Scripture. This isn't a recommendation; it's crucial. If we desire to be attuned to His voice, then we need to be rooted in His Word.

Period.

In Revelation 1:12-20, John recounts an encounter where he sees Jesus in heavenly splendour. John describes Jesus as having hair as white as snow and eyes like fire. His feet were like refined brass and His voice sounded as rushing waters. Out from Jesus' mouth came a double-edged sword. I believe the double-edged sword symbolizes both the *rhema* and *logos* word of God, co-labouring together as the full word of God. Every one of us needs to be completely rooted in the written Word of God and completely engulfed in the spoken word of God—not one or the other.

Scripture is an amazing gift that God has given us. If we want to keep in alignment with the path that God has ordained for us, we would be wise to study the roadmap that's been offered to us.

Here is a simple exercise for you to practice hearing God's voice through Scripture:

Depending on the person, this exercise will be most effective either through verbally speaking or through journaling. Feel free to do whichever you feel will help you best.

1. *Still your heart and mind.*
2. *Pick one of the following verses: (If you desire, you can choose to do this with all of them.)*
   - *Proverbs 3:5-6: "Trust in the Lord with all your heart, and lean not on your own understanding; in all your ways acknowledge Him, and He*

shall direct your paths."

- *Jeremiah 29:11: "For I know the thoughts that I think toward you, says the Lord, thoughts of peace and not of evil, to give you a future and a hope."*
- *Psalm 139:13-14: "For You formed my inward parts; You covered me in my mother's womb. I will praise You, for I am fearfully and wonderfully made; marvelous are Your works, and that my soul knows very well."*

3. Once you've chosen a verse, read it out loud or write it down.
4. Ask God, either verbally or through writing, "What is it that you want to speak to me through this verse?"
5. Pay attention to the flow of Holy Spirit within you. Pay attention to spontaneous God thoughts that enter your mind.
6. Record what you feel God tells you.
7. Test the word. Remember that God will speak words to you that will build up, encourage, and comfort you. (1 Thessalonians 5:20-21, says, "Do not despise prophecies. Test all things; hold fast what is good.")
8. If you didn't hear anything, don't be discouraged. Give yourself grace. Try this exercise another time, using different verses that are highlighted to you.

The Still, Small Voice

Even though the still, small voice of God might seem like the least extreme or supernatural way to hear Him speak, I believe it is one of the most common. Many believe that if God were to speak, He would do so audibly in order to get His point across. Although He may do this, I believe we are a people who God wants to be so close with in friendship that we will hear even His faintest of whispers.

1 Kings 19:11-12: "Then [God] said, 'Go out, and stand on the mountain before the LORD.' And behold, the LORD passed by, and a great and strong wind tore into the mountains and broke the rocks in pieces before the LORD, but the LORD was not in the wind; and after the wind an earthquake, but the LORD was not in the earthquake; and after the earthquake a fire, but the LORD was not in the fire; and after the fire a still small voice."

When we walk intimately with the Lord, our ears are tuned to discern Holy Spirit's voice from our own thoughts.

A lot of the time when we receive prophetic words through the still, small voice, it will come as a spontaneous *God-thought*. We need to learn to pull on that inspired thought by faith until it becomes a prophetic word. We tend to elevate rational thought above spontaneity. Rational thought isn't wrong; however, we can't lean on our own understanding. God wants us to lean on *His* understanding. We would be wise to remember that spontaneous God-thoughts are the river of Holy Spirit flowing within us.

John 7:37-39: "On the last day, that great day of the feast, Jesus stood and cried out, saying, 'If anyone thirsts, let him come to Me and drink. He who believes in Me, as the Scripture has said, out of his heart will flow rivers of living water.' But this He spoke concerning the Spirit, whom those believing in Him would receive; for the Holy Spirit was not yet given, because Jesus was not yet glorified."

I'll share a story with you concerning how God can use spontaneous thought to speak to us:

Before I share, I need to be honest with you. Dispersed throughout this book are numerous evangelistic stories of God moving beyond the four walls of the church. While each story is precious to my heart, and I believe precious to God, I found myself hesitant to include them. My hesitancy came from a concern of people mistaking me, believing I'm more than I am. I'm not an overtly bold person. Those who know me well understand that I'm very quiet and highly introverted. I have many friends who are far bolder than me. Thankfully, a quiet personality isn't a barrier for Holy Spirit. He can use anyone; He is simply looking for a yielded yes. Without Jesus, I am not bold; with Him, I am.

Several years ago, I was browsing through a bookstore. I wasn't trying to listen to God in that moment per se, but when I saw a man sitting at a table by himself, I could feel Holy Spirit prompting me to give him a prophetic word.

Walking up to him, I introduced myself, then said, "I believe that God speaks today, and I feel like He has a message for you."

At this point, I didn't have a word to give. However, isn't this just like God, to have us step out, trusting Him in faith?

The man looked at me skeptically, then said, "If God is real, then I would love a message from Him."

Suddenly the word "son" sang through my mind. This word didn't resound loudly; it was a God-thought.

I stepped out with that one word by faith, believing it would manifest into a word for him from the Father's heart. When we step out with the little, God rewards us with much.

I said, "I feel like God just told me that you have two sons, and that for the past two weeks, you've been lying awake at night, daydreaming about having more of an emotional connection with your youngest son. I feel like God is saying that you are going to notice a drastic change in how your son connects with you in these next few months."

The man had tears in his eyes. Through emotion-filled stutters, he told me that everything I said was true.

The word "business" then passed through my mind. By faith, I pulled on the word, saying, "I feel like God is saying that you have a call to business over your life. You've tried to start several businesses in the past fifteen years, but they didn't turn out the way you'd hoped. In fact, you've recently felt frustrated and stuck because you didn't see the desire of your heart come to pass."

I then said, "You are wanting to start a construction business in fine carpentry, aren't you?"

He nodded his head, shocked.

I said to him, "In these next six months, you are going to meet two Christian men who are going to want to help you start up your business. God is saying that you can trust them because He trusts them."

I watched this man's encounter with the voice of God shift his heart. This message was instrumental in his salvation. Notice how this was a detailed and accurate word about his life, yet it didn't come through an audible voice from God—although He can speak in such ways. This word didn't come from an angel or a dream—although He can do that as well. God spoke through a thought process.

We would be wise to remember that Holy Spirit isn't an *external* God. Therefore, we can't expect Him to only speak audibly. He is an *internal* God. He is closer than our skin, abiding within the depths of who we are. For this reason, He will use things such as our thought processes and impressions to communicate. When we walk intimately with the Lord, our ears are tuned to discern the gentle whisper of Holy Spirit.

We need to be a people who will allow God to fine-tune our ears to hear the word of the Lord, even if He is speaking in His faintest whisper.

Here is an exercise to help you in hearing God's voice through the still, small voice:

1. *Still your heart and mind.*
2. *Either verbally or through journaling, ask God this question: "God, if you were to play a game with me, what game would you play?"*
3. *Once you hear something, then ask Him, "How does this apply to my life? How do you want to encourage me through this?"*

4. *Allow your mind to tune to the spontaneous God thoughts that enter your mind.*
5. *Test the word. (Remember that God is only going to speak words that will build up, encourage, and comfort you.)*

Visions

I'm going to say a bold statement, one which would likely shake religious mentalities: *Vision* should be a prominent part of Christianity.

Why do I say this? It's because vision was a prominent part of Jesus' life.

John 5:19-20: "Most assuredly, I say to you, the Son can do nothing of Himself, but what He sees the Father do; for whatever He does, the Son also does in like manner. For the Father loves the Son, and shows Him all things that He Himself does; and He will show Him greater works than these, that you may marvel."

The entirety of Jesus' ministry on the earth was the by-product of what He saw the Father do in visions. It permitted what burned in the heart of the Father to be made manifest through the hands of the Son. We see in Scripture that vision wasn't reserved only for Jesus; it's for us as sons and daughters of God.

Acts 2:17: "And it shall come to pass in the last days, says God, that I will pour out of My Spirit on all flesh; your sons and your daughters shall prophesy, your young men shall see visions, your old men shall dream dreams."

Vision is a loaded topic, one that I will be elaborating on in chapter four. Considering how foundational it is for hearing God's voice, I must scratch the surface before moving on. While some visions can be dramatic—such as God opening our natural eyes to view spiritual things clearly—they can also be subtle. Remember, Holy Spirit isn't an *external* God; He is *internal*. Therefore, a vision can be as simple as God showing us a picture on the screen of our mind. Daniel 7:15 describes Daniel being troubled by the visions in his head, which tells us that the realm of visions can take place in the mind. Even a gentle picture in our mind can be a vision from the Lord.

I can still remember one of my first ministry trips; I was twenty years old. When I recall my earlier years in ministry, I often find myself cringing, remembering my inexperience—my overconfidence. I then am overtaken by thankfulness that God doesn't look for the experienced; He looks for the willing, proving His strength through our weaknesses. What a humbling honour it is to be used by God.

During this ministry trip, as I always did before speaking, I set aside time with the Lord to ask Him what He had planned for that particular church service. Days before the gathering, I walked down a dirt road in the backcountry, preparing my heart to listen. Immediately, He began to speak; however, His words didn't come in the still, small voice; nor was my mind illuminated with Scriptures. Instead, I saw a vibrant picture in my mind.

In this vision, it looked as though I could see into heaven. I saw a spear that glowed in eternal splendour, lightning bolts dancing all over it. I watched as the spear shot from heaven, cracking throughout the skies like a golden bolt. The spear met its mark, hitting the church where I was going to be speaking.

Days later, I arrived at the church. While speaking, I didn't mention what the Lord had shown me along the dirt road. As I went on sharing my message, the atmosphere was electric, not by my own doing. There was a woman on the other side of the sanctuary. She stood worshipping when she looked out the window beside her. Suddenly, she let out a yelp, dropping to the ground. This woman lay on the ground in an encounter with Jesus.

It was enough to make the place go into pandemonium. God began touching bodies, bringing healing. One after another, we watched Jesus transform hearts, souls, and bodies. All of this began with one woman who fell under the power of God.

After about one hour, the woman finally rose to her feet. I asked her, "What happened when you fell to the ground?"

She said, "It was the strangest thing: I looked out the window when all of a sudden it looked like I saw a golden lightning bolt shoot from the heavens. It shot through the sky, into the church, and hit me!"

She continued, "I came here tonight in excruciating pain from a migraine that I've had for half of a year; however, when that lightning bolt touched me, I was completely healed!"

All of this began from one vision—one imprint in my mind.

What if I told you that vision is supposed to be a consistent part of your walk with God? What if I told you that God can use it to connect you to the Father, just as it did with Jesus?

Proverbs 3:5-6: "Trust in the Lord with all of your heart, and lean not on your own understanding; in all your ways acknowledge Him, and He shall direct your paths."

One of the things that moves me profoundly about how Jesus only did what He *saw* His Father do, is that it reveals His humility. Jesus, the Son of God, in His humanity, knew that He couldn't lean on His own understanding. He needed the Father to show Him a better way. If Jesus modelled a life of humility and reliance upon the Father in such a way, then how much more should we? If His strategy was *vision*, then we would be wise to model our lives in such a way.

Here is an exercise to help you in hearing God's voice through vision:

---

1. *Still your heart and mind.*
2. *Either verbally or through journaling, ask God this question: "God, can you show me a vision concerning the calling that is written over my life?"*
   - *God may choose to speak to you through the still, small voice. Even so, press in for vision.*
   - *Vision may come as a glimpse in your mind. It may come more dramatically.*
3. *Trust Holy Spirit's leading. Let Him guide your thoughts and imagination.*
4. *Test the word. (Remember that God is only going to speak words that will build up, encourage, and comfort you.)*

For some of you reading, perhaps you've already been practicing hearing the voice of God for many years. Or, maybe you consider yourself new to hearing Him. I believe that there are no experts in God's kingdom. We are all learning, growing, maturing, and further tuning our ears to hear He who speaks everlasting life. Despite your level of experience, imagine living a life where God's voice isn't rare but common. The truth is that you weren't created to be a reed that bends by the slightest of opposition. You were fashioned to be rooted in His written Word and promises, where you can stand firm like an immovable cedar tree. You weren't meant to wander through life aimless and purposeless. You were designed to be guided by the voice of God, directed by Him like the wind catching a ship's sails.

You, my friend, were born to hear God.

God has given you the ability to partner with the prophetic promises over your life through declaration.

Chapter Three
Speaking Forth

I was sitting in a coffee shop when two women who were sitting at a nearby table caught my attention. Tarot cards were scattered all over the table between them, and I immediately realized that one of the women was a psychic in the middle of a reading.

Seeing this, my heart broke for the woman who was receiving the reading. Here she was, longing for a word from the Father but she didn't know it; therefore, she was settling for the counterfeit. She was crying out for *life* but was settling for *death*.

I remember saying to God, "Lord, what are you going to do?"

He returned the question by saying, "What are *you* going to do?"

Isn't that just like God?

Holy Spirit drew my attention to a man sitting at a nearby table next to the two women. I felt led to pray for him and give him a word from God's heart.

Walking over, I introduced myself. He seemed reluctant to let me pray for him but agreed nonetheless. With my hand on his shoulder, I prayed that God would touch his heart and I began to speak prophetically into his life. All of a sudden, this man who didn't know God began to feel His presence, causing him to spill over in uncontrollable laughter. While he laughed, he began shouting out, thanking God for touching his heart. In all honesty, I didn't expect such a dramatic display in the middle of a coffee shop. I was just as surprised as he was.

Looking at the table next to me, my eyes met the gaze of the psychic. I could hear her muttering to the woman sitting across from her. She said, "Ever since that man came near us, I haven't been able to read your fortune. It's as though my physic link has been severed."

The psychic stood up angrily, cast me a final cold glare, and then stormed out of the coffee shop. Since the woman who was doing the tarot card reading had left, this gave space for me to go and minister prophetically to the other woman. She no longer had to settle for the counterfeit. As I spoke words of life into her, she broke down in tears. She'd finally received what she was longing for: an encounter with the love of God.

This encounter from several years ago taught me something profound. This woman was starving for a word from God—for an encounter with a loving Father. Since she didn't know where to find Him, she turned to darkness. She settled for death instead of life. We face the very same choice. What have we tuned our ears to hear?

What have we allowed our mouths to speak? Are we proclaimers of death or life?

Proverbs 18:21: "Death and life are in the power of the tongue, and those who love it will eat its fruit."

I know a public school teacher who once did an experiment with his students. What he did was he kept a plant at his desk. He wouldn't give the plant any water or sunlight. Instead, they would feed the plant with words. Every day before class would start, he and his students would declare that the plant would die. They would decree death. They did this for three consecutive days. The plant, not receiving water, predictably would wither, dying. Once the plant was dead, they then declared every day for three days that the plant would live. Lo and behold, on the third day the plant came back to life! They would do this again and again. They killed and raised this plant from the dead a total of five times simply through declaration. What an incredible lesson for those students concerning the power of our words.

We would be amazed if we understood how directly linked our lives are to the words we speak. If we are speaking death, then that is exactly what we will reap. What if we chose to speak life? What if we could shift circumstances with our words? What if we allowed our tongues to be bound to the heart of the Father, declaring what He longs for?

Speaking to Storms

Most of us know the story of David and Goliath how the underdog took down the looming giant. Even though David wasn't yet the king of Israel, he was a king in God's eyes. In fact, God saw the heart of a king in David long before there was even a crown on his head. We know of how David's heroics shielded Israel from the Philistines; however, we often overlook an interesting detail. We remember David's sling and stone, but we forget about his decree. We forget about how he wielded the power of the tongue.

1 Samuel 17:45-46: "Then David said to the Philistine, 'You come to me with a sword, with a spear, and with a javelin. But I come to you in the name of the LORD of hosts, the God of the armies of Israel, whom you have defied. This day the Lord will deliver you into my hand, and I will strike you and take your head from you.'"

David uses his mouth to decree. When the king decrees something, it is established. David decreed the death of Goliath before he was even confronted. Goliath was a dead man before a stone even touched him. Israel faced a storm that came in the form of a giant; therefore, David used words as a weapon of warfare.

Job 22:28: "You will also declare a thing, and it will be established for you; so light will shine on your ways."

We can see Jesus moving in the power of words throughout His ministry:

Mark 4:35-39: "On the same day, when evening had come, He said to them, 'Let us cross over to the other side.' Now when they had left the multitude, they took Him along in the boat as He was. And other little boats were also with Him. And a great windstorm arose, and the waves beat into the boat, so that it was already filling. But He was in the stern, asleep on a pillow. And they awoke Him and said to Him, 'Teacher, do You not care that we are perishing?' Then He arose and rebuked the wind, and said to the sea, 'Peace, be still!' And the wind ceased and there was a great calm."

I will share a personal—and wild—story with you about the power of our words:

Several years ago, I was ministering in a specific city. The Lord began sharing with me through the still, small voice. He said, "I'm releasing a new wave of leaders in this city. Winds of transition are blowing. A sign of this word coming to pass is that a tornado is going to touch down in the city in the Spring of 2011 and not one person will be harmed."

I shared the word I received with a few trusted friends and leaders. Doing research on this particular city, I realized quickly that tornados weren't even remotely common. In fact, the last tornado that took place in the city was in 1973!

Almost forty years later, in the Spring of 2011, a tornado hit the city. Instead of landing near homes, it landed in a small park that was vacant of people. The tornado tore through the isolated area, and not a person was harmed. The exciting thing about this wasn't the sign of a tornado, but rather the manifestation of the word coming to pass: new leaders being appointed. The winds of transition were truly blowing. A city was being brought into God's order.

Almost seven years later, I was going to be ministering again in this very city. Leading up to this time, I had a fascinating dream.

I'm an avid dreamer and a keen believer that dreams are a common avenue that God chooses to speak (Job 33:15-16). In all honesty, I toyed with teaching on dreams in this book; however, God speaking in the night season deserves to be unpacked much more thoroughly. The topic deserved undivided attention in its own book. If you're interested in how God speaks through dreams, I would encourage you to read my book *Unlocking the Language of Dreams*.

In this particular dream, I saw the city; however, the atmosphere was dark. Four black funnel clouds hovered in the skyline as one tornado tore through the city. It caused catastrophic damage to homes and businesses.

Awaking from this dream, I did research again. I quickly learned that the only recently documented tornado in the city was the previous one that took place in the Spring of 2011.

Arriving in the city, I drove on my way to a meeting. The skies were blue, with no clouds in sight. There were no warnings concerning the weather for upcoming days—I checked. During my drive, the Lord then spoke to me, saying, "Another tornado is going to hit this city. While last time, a tornado was used as a sign and wonder, this time it has the potential to bring catastrophic damage to the city. This can be prevented by prayer and declaration."

I contacted several intercessors I knew, sharing with them my dream, and asked them to be praying for the city. The very next day—out of nowhere—dark clouds rolled into the city. Four massive funnel clouds hovered over the city, just as I saw in my dream, and tornado warnings were on nearly every radio station. It was only a few hours later that the tornado touched down.

I remember that day clearly. I drove out to the country with the intention to pray. The winds were wild—funnel clouds were thick and unwavering.

Amidst the storm, I remembered the words that God spoke to me in the dream: "This can be prevented by prayer and declaration." By faith, I began to pray and declare. I knew that there were many others who were doing so as well.

It wasn't long after that the tornado lifted. The funnel clouds broke apart. The winds ceased. No homes were wrecked. No people were harmed or injured. I truly believe that a city was protected because people were praying and speaking in authority.

This is a rather dramatic story that no doubt demonstrates the power of our words; however, you might be thinking, "How does this apply to me?"

It applies to you because your life is shaped by your words. God has given you the power to speak to storms in your life, decreeing the very word of God. Not only has He given you authority to stop the enemy, but also to shape your future. God has given you the ability to partner with the prophetic promises over your life through declaration.

Partnering with Promise

Understanding the power of words is a prominent part of the prophetic ministry. It's understanding this truth that bridges us beyond the place of viewing prophecy to only confirm. There is no doubt that prophecy confirms; however, it also speaks things into being. All of creation was brought forth through declaration. God didn't think, *let there be light*. He declared it, and it was so.

A story from 1 Samuel 1 tells of a man named Elkanah. Elkanah had two wives whose names were Hannah and Peninnah. Peninnah bore children for Elkanah whereas Hannah was barren. Hannah would go to the house of the Lord once a year to worship. One time while worshipping, she wept in anguish because of her barrenness. She made a vow, saying, "O LORD of hosts, if You will indeed look on the affliction of Your maidservant and remember me, and not forget Your maidservant, but will give Your maidservant a male child, then I will give him to the LORD all the days of his life, and no razor shall come upon his head" (1 Samuel 1:11).

The priest Eli noticed her weeping and blessed her saying, "Go in peace, and the God of Israel grant your petition which you have asked of Him," (1 Samuel 1:17).

It came to pass that Hannah conceived a child and named him Samuel. Samuel's life and his entire ministry were the fruit of the priest Eli's declaration of life.

I remember one time while being in a season of hiddenness. I knew that I was called to speak, minister, and write books. Doors hadn't yet opened and people around me didn't see my calling. Looking back, I know I wasn't even remotely ready for the work that God had planned for me. However, I found myself greatly discouraged. I was tormented by questions such as, "What if I didn't hear God right? What if I'm not called? What if I've already missed my opportunity?" These are questions that I'm sure many of us have faced and can relate to.

One day, I was in my home, and I knew I was at a tipping point. I could either give in to hope deferred becoming stagnant, or I could choose to stand in faith, making the decision to persevere.

I got down on my face before the Lord. I cried out to Him, asking Him for faith to believe in the prophetic promise over my life. I then began to speak out loud, declaring who I knew God told me I was created to be. This was a defining moment for me. I hadn't only heard God's word; I was partnering with His word.

This prompts some questions: What do you speak over your life? What do you speak over your home? What do you speak over your marriage and children? What do you speak over your business or finances? What do you speak over your calling? Do your words match your promises?

For the Israelites, it was their words that became the stronghold preventing them from stepping into promise. Once freed from the bondage of Pharaoh, the Israelites wandered in the wilderness. Even though they were free, they grumbled and complained. God eventually allowed them to live by their words, saying in Numbers 14:28: "Say to them, 'As I live,' says the LORD, 'just as you have spoken in My hearing, so I will do to you.'" By the Israelites' very words, that particular generation didn't enter the promised land. An entire generation died in the wilderness by their words, so that an upcoming generation would enter the promised land instead.

God's heart is that you will experience every promise He has spoken over your life. A part of seeing promise coming to pass is co-labouring with God, by making sure our words are in correct alignment. We need to learn to speak life over ourselves.

In closing this chapter, let me ask you something: When you look in the mirror, what do you see? Do you see someone who has been dealt a tough hand in life? Do you see yourself through the lens of your hurts, mistakes, or history?

When the Father looks at you, He doesn't look through the lens of your circumstances. He doesn't see you through your perceived weaknesses or shortcomings. He sees you through the lens of the blood of His Son, Jesus. Speaking life over ourselves is imperative to renewing our minds in what the Father says.

I want to lead you right now to take a moment to practice the power of declaration. I want to lead you in taking time to speak a blessing over yourself. You may want to spend time reading this over yourself daily, allowing it to penetrate your heart.

As you read these words, don't just *read* them. Speak them. And don't just *speak* them; believe them. Let them sink into your heart. Let them change the way that you see yourself.

Say this:

"I am significant. I am important. I am valuable. I am precious. I am priceless. I am loved by my heavenly Father. He believes in me. He is proud of me. He has created me for a divine reason. I have a calling and a destiny. I wasn't fashioned for the mediocre; I was created for purpose."

Activation

1. Spend time reflecting on some of the prominent prophetic promises that are over your life:
   - What has God spoken to you about your relationships?
   - What has God spoken about your finances?
   - What has God spoken over your marriage?
   - What has God spoken over your children, either current or future?
   - What has God spoken about your calling?
2. Spend time reflecting on your attitude towards these promises. Are you full of faith? Are you discouraged? Do you have hope deferred?
3. Considering your heart posture, what is your verbal dialogue (both auditory and internal)? Do you speak life over these different spheres of your life? Are there areas where you speak death?
4. Take time praying through each sphere of life, asking God to help bind your tongue to His purposes for your life.

Dr. Luc Niebergall

Prayer

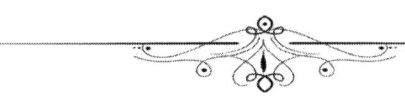

Pray this with me:

"Lord, I thank You that You've made it a kingdom principle that words have power. I thank You that my words carry authority. Forgive me for any times that I've spoken death when I should have spoken life. Forgive me for times when I've spoken death over others, including myself. I pray that You bind my tongue to Your heart. Teach me to prophesy what burns in Your heart, Lord."

"*Amen.*"

In this time, God is opening eyes to see.

Chapter Four
Vision

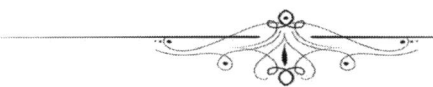

I can still remember the first time I saw an angel. I was eighteen years old at the time, in a remarkable season of learning to encounter God as my friend. As I would read through the Bible, I would be moved by stories of God sending angels to give messages to men and women. Having only known the Lord for two years, I thought things such as angels were fairytales, yet this holy book was telling me otherwise. I figured surely if God could reveal such things to others, then He could for me. I prayed for God to open my eyes to see.

I was out camping. Sitting around the campfire, I felt the whisper of Holy Spirit saying, "At 3:00 a.m., step outside the tent."

I wrestled with knowing if this was the Lord—as many of us would. Was what I'd heard just a fleeting thought, or was it truly God? If it was, what would be the purpose of leaving my tent?

As night dawned, I lay awake. Keeping my eye on my watch, I waited for 3:00 a.m. When the time came, I rose from my bed and exited the tent. In the dark of night, I remember feeling the cool wind as I walked to a nearby ridge. Staring into an ensemble of trees, I could see a pathway on the other side. I watched for a time, waiting, not knowing what to expect. That was when I saw it.

I watched as the path behind the trees flooded with light. Then I saw what appeared to be a man, clothed in linen robes. The angel slowly walked down the pathway, the brilliance of its heavenly splendour making it impossible to distinguish its features. This was the moment when I came to realize that angels aren't fairytales; they are very real.

I've just whetted your appetite with a story, but we can't camp out in only testimonies. We need theology. We need to understand how these supernatural occurrences are biblical. Whether it's seeing visions in our minds or seeing in the spirit realm, we need to understand how *vision* is biblical.

I am going to start this teaching off with a radical statement: You are a triune being.

In Genesis 1:26, God spoke, saying, "Let Us make man in Our image, according to Our likeness." God who is a Trinity—Father, Son, and Holy Spirit—fashioned us as body, soul, and spirit. Let's talk for a moment about our *spirit*. Our spiritual identity echoes all the way back to the beginning, in the Garden of Eden.

When Adam was created, he was shaped first from the dust of the earth (Genesis 2:7). He was formed by something of the *natural realm*. Since he was created of physical substance, he was given five natural senses. He was given natural senses to see, hear, touch, taste, and smell. In the very same verse, God then breathes into Adam the breath of life. *Breath of life* translated from its original language means "spirit." In this moment, Adam was no longer a man made of solely natural substance; he was also created of spirit. He had a spiritual identity.

Since he was born of *spirit*, Adam also had spiritual senses to experience God and the spiritual realm around him. Adam lived in two realms at the exact same time, being in a constant awareness of his natural and heavenly surroundings. Just as Adam could see birds and trees with his natural senses, he could also experience God and the angels. His day-to-day life consisted of tasting and seeing heavenly realities. Adam and Eve were flawless in body, soul, and spirit, bearing the unveiled image of God.

Once Adam and Eve ate from the *tree of the knowledge of good and evil*, they gave up their rights to live in their complete rights as a son and daughter of God. They lost understanding of their spiritual identity. Everyone who was born into this world after Adam and Eve was born into a lineage of death. For thousands of years, mankind lived in a spiritual drought. Although there were many who had relationship with God, it was one bridged through the *Law*. It was a relationship fostered without a revelation of spiritual identity. We needed a Saviour to come and redeem everything that was lost.

Luke 1:35: "And the angel answered and said to [Mary], 'The Holy Spirit will come upon you, and the power of the Highest will overshadow you; therefore, also, that Holy One who is to be born will be called the Son of God.'"

This verse reveals to us the parallel in how Adam and Jesus were created. In order to fashion Adam, God took something from the natural realm (dust of the earth) and something from heaven (the breath of life). For Jesus, in the same way, God took Mary—who was of the natural realm—and when the Spirit of the Lord came over her, the power of the Highest overshadowed her. In that moment the *spiritual seed* of heaven came together with the *natural egg* of Mary and Jesus was conceived. Jesus was the second man in all of history to be born not only as a natural man but also one who could live out His spiritual identity.

Jesus chose to partake of the *tree of life* for all of His days. He didn't sway as Adam had. Jesus' flawless surrender to the Father permitted Him to be the "last Adam," fulfilling what Adam could not. When we receive Holy Spirit upon salvation, the pure Spirit of Christ comes, becoming one with our lifeless spirit. We become born anew, not only born of body and soul but also ones who can live out our spiritual identity.

Acts 1:8: "But you shall receive power when the Holy Spirit has come upon you; and you shall be witnesses to Me in Jerusalem, and in all Judea and Samaria, and to the end of the earth."

When Holy Spirit comes upon us, we will receive power and become *witnesses*. What does it mean to become a witness? We often equate witnessing to preaching the gospel; however, witnessing has nothing to do with our mouths. Witnessing is about seeing!

Why, then, seek vision? It's not only about experiencing the supernatural; it's about living out our blood-bought spiritual identity. It's about experiencing

God and enjoying the benefits of the cross. It's about living how Jesus lived (John 5:19-20). Through the cross, Jesus restored us so that we wouldn't be limited in our identity. We are made complete in Him in body, soul, and spirit.

What an amazing reality it is to be born again.

Understanding Angels

Angels were crucial in Scripture; they are crucial in present times. Since I have such a focus in my ministry on training people to hear the voice of God, I've written extensively about seeing in the spirit realm. I've written much about angels. I tend not to shy away from repeating my revelations and stories in my writings. In fact, much of this chapter also appears in a book I wrote on spiritual warfare called *Warrior*. In order for us to learn, repetition is important. Our minds need to be renewed and soaked in truth.

Many become uncomfortable at the mention of angels. The truth is that God still uses angels to speak and minister. They are a part of God's kingdom. We are called to "seek first the kingdom" (Matthew 6:33). We seldom get uncomfortable with teachings concerning other aspects of God's kingdom such as peace and joy, so why, then, would we be leery of angels? Considering how frequently they are mentioned in Scripture, not believing in angels and their interaction with mankind is unbiblical.

Acts 8:26: "Now an angel of the Lord spoke to Philip, saying, 'Arise and go toward the south along the road which goes down from Jerusalem to Gaza.'"

Hebrews 1:14 says, "Are [angels] not all ministering spirits sent forth to minister for those who will inherit salvation?" I think we would be astounded if we truly understood the implications of this verse. Whether we believe it or not, there are angels assigned to our lives to minister to us. Right now, in this very moment, there are angels assigned to you, ministering to you.

One time, while teaching at a church, I began sharing testimonies about different encounters I've had with angels. While speaking, I watched those who were listening, when the pastor's wife caught my eye. She was, at the time, a very conservative woman not accustomed to the supernatural things of the Spirit.

Halfway through my message, while I was mid-sentence, I watched her quickly shuffle down one of the pews. She wasn't simply changing seats; it looked as though she was trying to get away from something. The look on her face told me that she was quite shaken. Trying not to become distracted, I tried my best to ignore her, continuing with my message.

At the end of the service, the pastor's wife walked up to me. She said, "I'm going to be honest with you. When you were teaching about angels, I was having a very hard time believing what you were saying. I decided to step out in faith. In my heart, I prayed, 'God, I don't know if angels are real. But if they are, and if Luc has experienced them, then surely so can I.'"

She went on to explain, "Right as those words escaped my mouth, I heard something behind me. Turning around, I saw an angel walk into the sanctuary. I've never seen anything like it before in my life. This angel sat down beside me. When it did, I was startled, so I shuffled down the pew. The angel followed me, shuffling as well. When I finally stopped, the angel leaned over to me and whispered the word of the Lord into my ear!"

It's stories like these that prod at me, causing me to desire to see the fullness of God's kingdom be made manifest in my life. There are numerous accounts of angels in the Bible, most of which involve interactions with mankind. In many instances, whenever there was something profound taking place in Scripture, angels were often mentioned. Remember the story of Peter's miraculous escape from prison, told in Acts 12. Peter leaves the jail and goes to the house where the other believers are praying for his escape. When he knocks on the door, a young girl named Rhoda comes, hears his voice, and runs to tell the others that Peter escaped. Notice the believers' response: they said to her, "You are beside yourself... It is his angel" (Acts 12:15), and then they continued praying.

Let me point something out here: these people believed that there was a physical manifestation of an angel knocking at their door and talking to a young girl, yet they brushed it off flippantly. This is how normal it was for the early church to experience God moving through angels. If the saints of old have died, then who else will they minister to other than you and me?

The Bible mentions a diverse embodiment of angels. One third of the angels fell with Satan (Revelation 12:4), meaning that there are twice as many angels as there are demons. We are quick to believe that there are demons (spirits) of lust, poverty, and anger. It only makes sense, then, that there would also be angels of purity, abundance, and joy. John 5 mentions a healing angel that would stir the pool of Bethesda; whoever would be the first to step in would be healed from any pain or infirmity. Most Biblical references of angels describe them as taking the form of males (Judges 13:6, Daniel 10:5-21); however, Zechariah 5:5-9 mentions two angels that were in the form of women with wings like storks. The author of Hebrews wrote in Hebrews 13:2, "Do not forget to entertain strangers, for by so doing some have unwittingly entertained angels."

After Jesus was tempted by the enemy in the desert, "the devil left Him, and behold, angels came and ministered to Him" (Matthew 4:11). If Jesus the Messiah allowed angels to minister to Him, then surely we can choose to be humble enough to receive their ministry.

Eyes to See Heaven

I'm one who frequently sees in the spirit, although I rarely make mention of what I see. Since I have influence not only with charismatic churches but also with those more conservative, I often keep my stories to a minimum concerning what I share. I reserve what I witness daily with those who are closest to me: my wife, close friends, and our spiritual sons and daughters. I share far more around tables than I do from stages.

I will, however, share this story with you. Not too long ago, I was ministering in a specific province in Canada. The night before I was to minister, I was with the hosts who had invited me and the other speakers. While conversing, the Lord spoke to me.

Feeling the weight of what He said, I excused myself from the table, making my way to my hotel room. I called my wife, saying to her, "Please pray for me. The Lord told me I'm going to have a dream tonight. This dream is going to be the word of the Lord for the region."

I went to sleep that night and had a profound dream. I knew that I was armed with a message from God's heart for the region. That morning, arriving at the church, I went up to speak.

With a hundred and fifty people in front of me, I asked, "Who here drove at least two hours to be here today?"

Sixty percent of the hands went up. Prodding further, I quickly realized that many drove four to six hours to be at the gathering. God had gathered the region to hear His word.

I said, "I had a dream last night, which is a word for this region."

Right as the words escaped my mouth, I looked up. It looked as though the sky had split open. I could see into heaven—into God's throne room. I could see Jesus seated on the throne. I could see seraphim flying about (Isaiah 6). Each was about one hundred feet in length. Each bearing six wings, two of their wings covered their faces in humility being in the presence of the Almighty. These angels didn't fly quickly, as a bird would. They moved remarkably slowly, like a whale swimming in deep waters. As I shared the dream, I watched as one of these grand angels dove from heaven into earth, into this sanctuary.

When we experience the supernatural in such a way, there should be tangible fruit. I wouldn't share this testimony unless there were. What happened next offended my natural mind.

One hundred and fifty people fell to their faces—I was the only one remaining standing. Some wept uncontrollably. Others screamed. This holy moment overtook the room. It was both terrifying and wonderful. In the presence of the Lord, I released the word of the Lord for the region. I believe we would be truly astounded if we understood what happens in the spirit realm when God moves.

2 Corinthians 4:18: "While we do not look at the things which are seen, but at the things which are not seen. For the things which are seen are temporary, but the things which are not seen are eternal."

Why is it that we should fix our eyes on the unseen? Well, let me ask you a few questions: When you read the story I just shared, did it begin to open your eyes to the reality of heaven? Did it build your faith in knowing that life is more than what we can see with our natural eyes? The truth is that when we fix our eyes on the unseen, it changes us. It reveals the reality of God's kingdom.

Scripture is filled with people seeing beyond the natural. Ezekiel saw the cherubim (Ezekiel 1). Isaiah witnessed the seraphim (Isaiah 6). John encountered the four living creatures (Revelation 4). Ephesians 1:3 says we are blessed with every spiritual blessing in the heavenly realms. This verse doesn't say we will *one day* be blessed with every spiritual blessing in the heavenly realms. We are blessed now. We are seated with Jesus now (Ephesians 2:6).

One of my favourite stories in Scripture about seeing in the spirit is the one of Elisha and his servant. Take a look at this with me:

2 Kings 6:16-17: "So [Elisha] answered, 'Do not fear, for those who are with us are more than those who are with them.' And Elisha prayed, and said, 'LORD, I pray, open his eyes that he may see.' Then the LORD opened the eyes of the young man, and he saw. And behold, the mountain was full of horses and chariots of fire all around Elisha."

It is interesting to me that the servant in this passage isn't Gehazi, who was Elisha's appointed apprentice. *Gehazi* translated from Hebrew means "valley of vision," which means "one who cannot see or perceive." I believe that we are living in a time when God is delivering many from an inability to see, perceive, and understand the supernatural realm around us. He is giving us vision like Elisha's new servant to perceive the spiritual war that is taking place.

Let's see how the story unfolds:

2 Kings 6:18: "So when the Syrians came down to him, Elisha prayed to the Lord, and said, 'Strike this people, I pray, with blindness.' And He struck them with blindness according to the word of Elisha."

In this story, we see the Lord opening the eyes of Elisha's servant and closing the eyes of the Syrians, who at the time were an enemy of Israel. The lesson from this story is that when we perceive the reality of heaven and the unseen, we renew our minds in our heavenly identity. When we stand in our birthright, the enemy is blinded to us. Abiding under the safety—the immunity—of the Lord is a part of our inheritance as sons and daughters of God.

I'm going to end this chapter with one last story:

Several years ago, I had a vision. I could see heaven all around me. I was walking down a road that looked as though it was made of stone. I walked for what seemed to be several hours when Holy Spirit drew my attention to the stone road that I was traveling. A sudden urge gripped me to lay my hand on the floor of heaven. I stopped mid-step, got down onto my knees, and began brushing my hand across the rocky street. Wonder took me when I saw that I was not walking on a road made of stone, but that the apparent grey rock was actually dust covering the streets of gold. The gold shone in absolute purity, mastered to perfection and incomparable to any type of metal that I had ever seen.

I asked Holy Spirit why the streets of gold were covered in dust. Responding, He said, "It is because not many people have walked where you are walking; however, that is about to change. Even though many have not yet walked here, I am releasing revelation to sons and daughters that they will know and understand their access to the kingdom of heaven.

"In this time, I am opening eyes to *see*."

Prayer

Pray this with me:

"Holy Spirit, I pray that You open my eyes to see. I pray that You activate vision in my life. Jesus, just as You saw everything that You saw the Father do, I pray for eyes to see. I ask for faith to believe in the reality of the kingdom of heaven. I pray that You activate my spiritual senses. I pray to witness visions from Your heart. I pray that You open my eyes to the spiritual realm around me.

"Amen."

Part II
The Four Revelatory Gifts

A predominant part of the prophetic ministry is to look at people through the eyes of heaven—through the eyes of the Father—and to speak that forth.

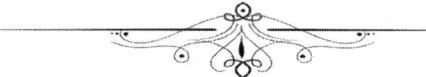

CHAPTER FIVE
Prophecy

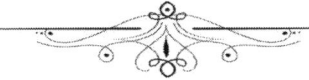

You aren't called to experience a mediocre life. Heaven isn't a reward for trudging through a depressing life; the benefits of heaven are a reward for what Jesus did on the cross! This means that you can live *in* purpose now. You were fashioned to impact hearts and lives around you. You were created to lead, walking out your unique calling and destiny in the Lord. This is why it's important for us to be equipped in the gifts of the Spirit.

Those who are experienced in hearing God's voice will often function in what I call the *four revelatory gifts*. Take a look at this:

1 Corinthians 12:7-11: "But the manifestation of the Spirit is given to each one for the profit of all: for to one is given the word of wisdom through the Spirit, to another the word of knowledge through the same Spirit, to another faith by the same Spirit, to another gifts of healings by the same Spirit, to another the working of miracles, to another prophecy, to another discerning of spirits, to another different kinds of tongues, to another the interpretation of tongues. But one and the same Spirit works all these things, distributing to each one individually as He wills."

Throughout the next few chapters, we will be looking at the revelatory gifts mentioned in the verses you just read:

- Prophecy
- Words of knowledge
- Messages of wisdom
- Discerning of spirits

Let's begin with prophecy.

Prophecy is to tap into the voice of God, speaking His word and heart to people, families, communities, cities, and nations. The prophetic ministry is a tool to speak God's word into people's callings, relationships, finances, seasons, and much more. A predominant part of the prophetic ministry is to look at people through the eyes of heaven—through the eyes of the Father—and to speak that forth. Prophecy reveals kingdom identity. It calls forth calling and destiny.

Prophets of the Old Testament were men and women who modelled utmost integrity. These pioneers in hearing God's voice whom we hold in the highest regard were unwavering in the word of the Lord; they were steadfast in their character. The modern prophetic ministry should exemplify no less.

With the amount of travelling, speaking, and training I've done surrounding the prophetic ministry throughout the years, to say I've witnessed a lot would be an understatement. There have been times when I've seen prophecy utilized with utmost integrity. I've seen how it can impact hearts, homes, cities, and nations. I've also seen it stewarded poorly. God doesn't *only* want a people who hear His voice; that is only half of the equation. He wants people who will hear Him in *health*. This is why protocol is imperative. Prophetic activation isn't enough; we need prophetic culture. Healthy prophetic culture won't bear dysfunction; it will reflect the character of God.

A prominent key to understanding how the gifts of the Spirit function is understanding that God is not divided in Himself. This means that the gifts of the Spirit mentioned in 1 Corinthians 12 will not contradict the fruits of the Spirit.

Galatians 5:22-23: "But the fruit of the Spirit is love, joy peace, longsuffering, kindness, goodness, faithfulness, gentleness, self-control. Against such there is no law."

Peppered throughout this chapter will be teachings not only on how to function in prophecy, but how to do so healthily. Since I've already given ample examples of prophetic words so far, this chapter will consist of teaching concerning protocol. The prophetic protocol that you are about to read has been compiled through years of experience in training people to hear the voice of God. It has developed from the premise that the gifts of the Spirit are meant to serve others and to demonstrate the heart of the Father. It was assembled remembering that Holy Spirit is true to His nature and that people are valuable.

Receiving a Word

The first facet we can look at concerning prophecy is how we *receive a word*. My heart, in many ways, is to take prophecy—which seems to be a complex topic—and to demystify it. In truth, it is quite simple to receive a prophetic word for someone. Psalm 139:17-18 says, "How precious also are Your thoughts to me, O God! How great is the sum of them! If I should count them, they would be more in number than the sand."

God has limitless good thoughts and affection towards each person. His thoughts towards us are so endless that they outweigh the grains of sand. All we need to do to encourage someone with a prophetic word is to tap into one of those thoughts.

We've talked about how we can hear from God through the still, small voice of God and through visions; however, how do we discern if what we are hearing is accurate? One of the most common questions I am asked when teaching people in the prophetic ministry is: How can I tell the difference between God's voice and my own thoughts?

This is a valid question, considering that there are different influences from the spirit realm that we can hear. As sons and daughters of God, we need to learn to distinguish the differences between the voice of Holy Spirit, our own internal voice, and the voice of the enemy.

I am going to give you some tips regarding how to receive a prophetic word for someone and to discern whether or not it is the voice of the Lord:

- Does the word line up with the Bible?

The prophetic word of God will always submit to the written word of God. The *rhema* submits to the *logos* because God will never contradict Himself. I always encourage people who are learning to prophesy to be adamant in their meditation of God's written word. The Bible is our plumb line revealing God's heart, nature, and character. We have a responsibility to be immersed in God's *logos* Word. If we ever feel that we hear anything prophetically that doesn't align with Scripture, then we carry the responsibility to disregard that word.

- Does the word edify, exhort, and comfort? (1 Corinthians 14:3)

While we may at times perceive the negative with our discernment, this should not prevent us from seeing the good and the potential in people. We want to speak life into people's lives. Truly being prophetic is to see past dysfunction and presumption and tap into who the person was created to be.

- Does the word line up with the character of God?

Remember, the nine gifts of the Spirit (1 Corinthians 12) will submit to the nine fruits of the Spirit (Galatians 5:22-23). If we receive a word that contradicts God's character, then we are to dismiss said word.

- Is the word by any means manipulative?

It is wise to observe our hearts when moving in the gifts of the Spirit. Am I wanting to prophesy over someone because I want something from them? If so, then my desire to prophesy isn't coming from a healthy place. The first reason why we should want to prophesy is to be obedient to God. Secondly, we should want to prophesy because we love the individual. If we aren't moved by genuine love towards someone, then we shouldn't be opening our mouths to prophesy.

- Does the word bear witness with our spirit?

We need to remember that the gifts of the Spirit work best from the place of friendship with God. For myself, I'm not content with just prophesying; I want to move in my gift in partnership with God. As I receive a word for someone, I want to make sure I feel the Lord's delight on it. Holy Spirit abides in us; therefore, if the word is from God, then He will testify to its validity.

1 Corinthians 2:10: "But God has revealed them to us through His Spirit. For the Spirit searches all things, yes, the deep things of God."

- Don't prophesy about dates, mates, or babies.

When I am developing a prophetic community in a church or ministry, I often set a standard rule that we shouldn't be prophesying about who people will marry, who they should date, or timelines for having children. The reason it is wise to veer away from these types of words is because they are so close to the heart. We are all students, still learning and growing in our ability to hear God's voice. With these more tender topics, I believe God wants to speak to us personally about them rather than through those who are still growing in their prophetic gift.

- Do not try to use someone's physical appearance as a template to receive a word for them.

We need to remember that God looks beyond what man sees. When Samuel was about to anoint David as king over Israel, God said to him, "Do not look at his appearance or at his physical stature, because I have refused him. For the LORD does not see as man sees; for man looks at the outward appearance, but the LORD looks at the heart" (1 Samuel 16:7).

Samuel was a mature prophet, yet God found it necessary to remind him of this. We need to remember that as prophetic people, we can see beyond what man sees. We can see others through the eyes of heaven.

Interpreting the Word

The second facet of prophecy is *interpreting the word*. Interpretation is often only necessary when God speaks through visions.

When God gives us a vision in our mind, we can proceed in asking Holy Spirit for an interpretation. Holy Spirit may give an interpretation, or He may not. Sometimes God won't reveal the interpretation to the person prophesying because the message is sensitive or intimate between Him and the recipient of the word. If He does not offer an interpretation, then we are to just share what the Lord showed instead of trying to fabricate an interpretation. We do not want to add on to what God has already said.

A dear friend of mine once shared a story with me. While praying with a woman, she was waiting upon the Lord. All of a sudden, she received a simple vision in her mind. It was a vision of a rubber ducky. She asked Holy Spirit for an interpretation of the peculiar vision. Holy Spirit went on to tell her that this picture was a personal word between Himself and the woman she was ministering to; therefore, He did not want to give her the interpretation.

My friend then shared with the woman the vision of the rubber ducky. The woman broke down sobbing. She explained how a rubber ducky was her favourite toy growing up and that it was what she would play with to distract her from the abuse that was taking place in her home. This simple vision was a pivotal key to this woman receiving healing in her heart.

Delivering the Word

Healthy prophetic delivery is important because a perfectly good word can be ruined by a poor delivery. We see this with Joseph's dream in Genesis 37:5-8. Joseph no doubt had a word from God; however, he spoke it forth with pride in his heart. This created a mess for himself.

Here are some tips concerning how to deliver a prophetic word properly:

- Let your attitude, tone, and character line up with the focus of the word God is speaking.

If I were to speak a word that is about the Father heart of God, I'm likely not going to raise my voice. I would be speaking gently because He is ministering to someone's heart. If I were to, say, prophesy about someone's calling, and I can feel the excitement of heaven, then I may allow my tone to match the excitement of heaven.

- Be yourself!

As you deliver a prophetic word, do not submit to any form of intimidation that says you need to look or sound like someone else while prophesying. God desires to use you just the way you are.

- Use language such as, "I feel like God is saying…" or "I sense that God is saying…"

Humility is essential. Some truths in Scripture are black and white. In these instances, we can declare away! However, when it comes to things more directional, such as people's callings and destinies, then it is wise to say, "I feel" or "I sense," rather than being unequivocal like, "God is saying…." This is honouring to the individual, to avoid them feeling trapped in the word that we are speaking to them.

- Ask for feedback.

When I train people to prophesy, I make it part of the culture to ask for feedback once they are finished giving a prophetic word. I do this for two reasons. The first reason is that it gives people an "out" if they feel it is an incorrect prophetic word. We should never manipulate people into embracing our prophetic word because we feel insecure about being wrong. It shows love to honour people by giving them an opportunity to share their opinion of the word. Secondly, we ask for feedback because if a part of our word is wrong, then we can fix it for the next time. That way, we can continually grow in our prophetic gift and delivery. A prophetic community can be a place where we learn to hone our gift.

Correctional Prophecy

People will often ask me what my thoughts are on correctional prophetic words. I do believe that there are times for correctional prophecy. I also believe that these types of words should be done with both order and integrity.

One place where correctional prophetic words function well is in the context of relationships. An example would be, say, since my wife and I are in a proven relationship, I have given her permission to speak into my life if Holy Spirit reveals something in my heart, life, or ministry that needs to be adjusted. It is our relationship that gives her this right in my life. I also have an accountability team consisting of trusted friends and leaders to whom I have given this level of trust.

Correctional prophetic words are merited if we are a leader and need to bring order into someone's life whom we are entrusted to lead. This should, of course, be executed in an honouring way. The same could be said if we are intentionally discipling someone and they have given us permission to bring correction to their life. I also know proven prophets who will receive correctional prophetic words. These men and women are trusted and faithful leaders who have learned to wield the word of the Lord throughout decades with integrity and honour.

I just listed several ways in which I believe correctional prophetic words are acceptable; I'm certain that there are many other scenarios where they are warranted. At the end of the day, God can speak however He chooses. What I am saying, however, is that correctional words should not be predominant in our prophetic expression. If a significant portion of our prophetic words are correctional, then there is a good chance that we are perceiving hearts, people, and scenarios through the wrong lens. God's heart isn't for prophecy to be an invasive and exposing ministry. We can't succumb to looking through a cynical or pessimistic lens. Our goal needs to be to see the way God sees.

Disregarding False Words

1 Corinthians 14:29: "Let two or three prophets speak, and let the others judge."

We have looked at how we can receive and deliver words for others; however, what if someone is prophesying over us? What is our responsibility?

When someone gives us a word, it is essential that we judge the word before we apply it to our lives. Not only is it essential, but it is actually our responsibility.

In the Old Testament, the full responsibility to discern the Lord's voice was on the person who spoke the word. The reason why the full weight of responsibility was on them was because Holy Spirit did not abide in man in the Old Testament. Therefore, people weren't able to discern what was God's word and what was not.

In new covenant times, when we are born again, we are filled with the Spirit of God. Therefore, we carry the ability to discern. We are responsible for what we receive as truth. We may not always be able to prevent someone from declaring something negative over us, but we are the ones who decide whether it affects our inner being.

When you are a leader, it is crucial to learn not to let people's words and opinions stick to you. You would be surprised at the gossip and slander that can take place about you when you're in leadership. You would be shocked by some of the negative and condemning "supposed prophetic words" people have given me throughout the years. Every time this happens, I make sure that I don't pull these words into my heart. I don't have time to renew my mind in lies. I also make a point to genuinely pray for the betterment of those who have talked badly of me. I do this so that they can be blessed and also so my heart won't be plagued with offence.

Some of you reading right now may have had negative words spoken over you. Those words may have been given by someone with a good heart, yet their word was not in line with what the Lord wants for your life. Or, perhaps the person may have spoken these things out of bitterness or offence to intentionally cause hurt. Either way, God doesn't want you to carry words that have brought you pain. If this applies to you, then please pray this prayer:

"Jesus, right now, I repent for allowing negative words to come into my heart. I wipe myself off from the lies of the enemy. I forgive those who have spoken negative words over my life. I choose to not submit to the weight of these words any longer. Holy Spirit, shower me with the truth of what the Father says about me. I am a child of God. My Father has grand plans for my life. I am protected by His love and by His truth. Thank you, Lord, that Your words over me are words of life, love, joy, and peace."

Prophetic Activation

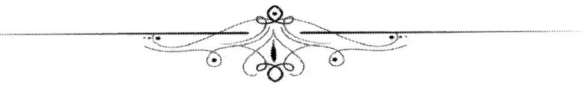

All the activations leading up to this point have revolved around hearing God for ourselves. Now, I want to lead you in receiving a prophetic word for someone else. Please follow these steps:

1. Find a quiet place. Tune your attention to Jesus.
2. Ask Holy Spirit to highlight someone to you.
3. Once Holy Spirit highlights someone to you, ask Him, "What do you want to show me about this person's calling?"
4. When you feel like you receive something, walk your word through the prophetic protocol in this chapter under Receiving a Word.
5. If you've received a vision, ask God if it requires interpretation.
6. Deliver the word following the protocol written in this chapter under Delivering the Word.

Words of knowledge can function like a key to unlock individuals' hearts, becoming a bridge for them to encounter Jesus.

Chapter Six
Words of Knowledge

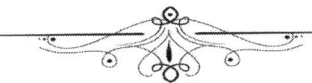

Several years ago, I took a young fellow whom I was mentoring to a store—he was fifteen years old. While conversing, I shared several healing testimonies I had experienced throughout my years of travelling and speaking. As each story passed, I witnessed a restlessness growing within him.

He finally piped up, saying, "Luc, I love your stories, but I want some of my own."

What a wonderful revelation. What would it look like if we understood that the testimonies of others could become launching pads of our own?

His faith stirred me, and I said, "Let's create some testimonies then."

Seeing two women in the makeup aisle, I walked towards them.

The young man followed. Approaching them, I said to the younger woman, "This might be a strange question, but do you by any chance have any pain in your body that you need healing from?"

She looked at me skeptically, replying, "No, not at all…"

I replied, "Are you sure you didn't hurt your left ankle while dancing two weeks ago?"

Her jaw dropped. "How did you know that?!" she asked.

I replied, "There is a God who loves you and knows everything about you."

I motioned to the young man with me, saying, "If you let my friend here pray for you, then God is going to heal your ankle."

My friend got down on his knees, laid his hands on her ankle, and prayed. After receiving prayer, she stepped down, and her ankle was completely healed! This young woman gave her heart to the Lord that night.

We made our way through the store. I moved in words of knowledge for healing while my young friend prayed for them. I'm not exaggerating in saying that we witnessed nearly twenty notable healings that evening. God used words of knowledge and healing to introduce Himself to many people that night. Close to twenty lives were transformed because of the faith of a young fifteen-year-old teenager who desired to be used by God.

While prophecy can be, in a sense, communicating the heart of God to an individual or even foretelling of what is to come, a word of knowledge is measured by *fact*. Words of knowledge consist of God revealing what has occurred or is occurring in someone's life rather than what may one day occur. In this story, when I asked the young woman about having hurt her ankle dancing two weeks prior, this wasn't prophecy; this was a word of knowledge.

Jesus often utilized words of knowledge throughout His ministry:

John 1:47-49: "Jesus saw Nathanael coming toward Him, and said of him, 'Behold, an Israelite indeed, in whom is no deceit!' Nathanael said to Him, 'How do You know me?' Jesus answered and said to him, 'Before Philip called you, when you were under the fig tree, I saw you.' Nathanael answered and said to Him, 'Rabbi, You are the Son of God! You are the King of Israel!'"

This story shows Jesus revealing details about Philip that He would not have known apart from revelation. Some might ask: What is the point of a word of knowledge like this? In this story in particular, what started with Jesus giving a word of knowledge resulted in Philip saying, "You are the Son of God!" Jesus' word of knowledge unlocked Philip's heart, inspiring him to glorify Jesus. This is why words of knowledge can be such a beneficial tool for a ministry such as evangelism. Words of knowledge can function like a key to unlock individuals' hearts, becoming a bridge for them to encounter Jesus.

Receiving Words of Knowledge

Words of knowledge function very well with gifts of healing. Time and time again, I've watched Jesus use a word of knowledge to build faith for healing, often resulting in salvation.

Here are some ways that people may receive words of knowledge for healing:

- The Lord may highlight either a part of our own body or someone else's.

Often, we dismiss the Lord speaking in this way because we assume that He should speak in more of a supernatural way. However, this is a common way that He will give words of knowledge for healing.

- We may feel a subtle sense of pain in our body that we have not felt before.

This can be a way that the Lord chooses to reveal the pain that someone else is experiencing.

- We may have the image of a body part light up in our mind.
- We may feel heat, coolness, or wind on a part of our body.

Here is an activation for you in stepping out for words of knowledge:

1. *With a few trusted people, plan a time when you can go to a place such as a shopping mall, grocery store, downtown, etc.*

2. *Before you go, as a group, spend some time waiting on the Lord. Ask God for words of knowledge for healing.*

3. *Pay attention to whether Holy Spirit is highlighting parts of your body. Is He giving you visions of people who need healing? Jot down what He is showing you.*

4. *As you go out, pay attention to who you are seeing. Is there anyone who fits the scope of what the Lord showed you in prayer? Is there anyone highlighted to you? Is God highlighting words of knowledge?*
5. *Step out in faith. In this stage, remember that this isn't about you witnessing the supernatural; it's about loving people well. Use words of knowledge as a bridge to administer healing, freedom, and the message of Jesus.*

I believe that Jesus walked in something greater than a word of knowledge gifting. He functioned in the *Spirit of knowledge.*

Isaiah 11:2: "The Spirit of the Lord shall rest upon Him [Jesus], the Spirit of wisdom and understanding, the Spirit of counsel and might, the Spirit of knowledge and of the fear of the Lord."

While ministering in words of knowledge, we may receive a limited amount of information. By ministering under the Spirit of knowledge, we can have a far broader understanding. Take a look at this:

John 2:24-25: "Jesus did not commit Himself to them, because He knew all men, and had no need that anyone should testify of man, for He knew what was in man."

"He knew what was in a man." This quote shows us Jesus' level of understanding concerning individuals. When I was much younger, the Lord brought me through an interesting season where He was training me in how to grow in supernatural *knowledge.* He led me, for example, to go to a restaurant with people after church that I didn't know. I would go from person to person, asking Holy

Spirit questions about them.

I would look at the first person and ask Holy Spirit, "In what ways have you gifted this person?" Once I received an answer, I would then do this with the second person, and then with the rest in the group.

I would then start again at the first person and ask Holy Spirit, "What season of life is this person in right now?" I would proceed with listening for everyone else in the group.

Starting with the first person again, I would then ask the Lord, "Can you speak to me about this person's calling and destiny?" I would proceed, doing the same with everyone else.

By the end, I would have a well-rounded understanding of who these people were, even if I'd had no previous interaction with them. Not only that, but I was training my eyes to see people the way that God sees them rather than through a temporal lens.

Throughout the gospels, we witness Jesus moving in an astounding knowledge of people, all by supernatural means. There are even records of Jesus knowing people's thoughts (Matthew 9:4, Matthew 12:25, Luke 5:22, Luke 6:8, Luke 11:17). Am I saying we should go around trying to "tap into" people's thoughts? Absolutely not. We need to be led by the Spirit—something that Jesus did flawlessly. What I am saying is that we've only scratched the surface. There is still so much about God's kingdom for us to understand.

As we hone our gifts—words of knowledge included—we need to make sure that we maintain a healthy heart posture. Our "why" is always important to God. Why am I trying to receive words of knowledge? Am I trying to seem spiritual? Am I curious about the supernatural? In my opinion, neither reason is sufficient. God doesn't gift us for our sake; He gifts us for the sake of others.

2 Chronicles 9:8: "Blessed be the Lord your God, who delighted in you [Solomon], setting you on His throne to be king for the Lord your God! Because your God has loved Israel, to establish them forever, therefore He made you king over them, to do justice and righteousness."

God didn't make Solomon king over Israel for his sake; He made Solomon king because He loved Israel, desiring a good leader to guide them. As we pursue the supernatural things of God, we need to have this understanding established in our hearts.

I'll be the first to admit that I'm still learning. In my early journey of hearing God's voice, I spent a lot of time learning to receive words of knowledge. While I was at times accurate, there were also moments when I was wrong. In this holy journey of falling on my face and learning to get back up again, I discovered an important key: I learned how to guard my *heart posture*.

I remember being nineteen years old. I had an unquenchable fire to see Jesus lavishing love upon the seemingly unlovable. Every day, I found myself either downtown or at hospitals, spending time with people and ministering to them.

One particular day, I found myself at a hospital. I saw a man sitting in a wheelchair, both of his legs bound in casts. I could immediately tell that he was very rough in personality. Through his tough exterior, I could see a man who was broken in heart. He felt cast on the outside of society. God wanted to touch his life.

I asked God, "Is there a word of knowledge you want to give me to share with him?"

Something came to mind; however, I felt unsure of the word. I took a leap of faith, nonetheless. Walking up to him, I introduced myself, sharing my *assumed* word of knowledge. I was immediately met with a blank stare, the word clearly inaccurate.

My heart for this man helped me to push past my embarrassment. I asked, "What happened to your legs?"

He was quick to share with me, saying, "I was partying two weeks ago and jumped off a balcony. When I landed on the pavement, both of my heels shattered."

"I believe that Jesus heals today. Can I pray for you?" I asked.

He didn't hesitate, saying, "Please, pray for me."

It still confounds me how starved people are for a touch from our loving God. I prayed a prayer of faith. Once finished, I invited him to rise from his wheelchair. As he did, the Lord gave him two brand-new heels! Tears streaming down his face, he gave his heart to Jesus. A man was healed and saved from an incorrect word of knowledge!

I walked away from this encounter with a teaching from the Lord. When a slave steps out and makes a mistake, they are punished for it. When a child of God steps out and makes a mistake, God makes it work out for good. This all comes down to heart posture. Why do we do what we do?

Pursuing the gifts of the Spirit from a place of wanting to edify ourselves is the by-product of orphanship. It is limited and lacks authority. In contrast, pursuing the gifts from the place of loving others is the fruit of sonship and daughterhood.

As we grow in the supernatural things of God, we carry a responsibility to make sure that our love for others always outweighs our gifting.

Conclusion

Words of knowledge aren't only limited to physical ailments. Moses moved powerfully in a gift of knowledge. Most theologians believe that Moses was the author of the first five books of the Bible, including Genesis. If this is true, then Moses must have received profound insight through divine revelation concerning events that took place before he was even born. I don't doubt that there must have been some form of documented history about what was recorded in Genesis. That said, I can't see how Moses would have written something such as the creation account in such detail without experiencing it himself through, say, visions and dreams.

We can see Jesus using words of knowledge for the purpose of bringing healing to a Samaritan woman's soul in the story of the woman at the well:

John 4:16-18: "Jesus said to [the Samaritan woman], 'Go, call your husband, and come here.' The woman answered and said, 'I have no husband.' Jesus said to her, 'You have well said, "I have no husband," for you have had five husbands, and the one whom you now have is not your husband; in that you spoke truly.'"

Here, we see Jesus using a word of knowledge, revealing that this woman had had five husbands. Jesus didn't do this to shame her; I believe He did this to free her from shame.

John 4:28-30: "The woman then left her waterpot, went her way into the city, and said to the men, 'Come, see a Man who told me all things that I ever did. Could this be the Christ?' Then they went out of the city and came to Him."

This woman's breakthrough didn't stop at transformation in her own life. She became a trumpet throughout her city, testifying of Jesus. All of this came from one Man exercising a word of knowledge. It came from her knowing that in the thick of her pain and trying life, God *saw* her.

I'll end this chapter with a story. Years ago, I was on an errand to a grocery store. Roaming through the aisles, I saw a worker stocking shelves. The Lord revealed to me that she suffered from pain in her lower back. In all honesty, I was tired. I wrestled with wanting nothing more than to just pick up what I needed and then head home. There was, however, something that prodded me: I could feel the Father's heart swelling for her.

I walked up to her and introduced myself. I then said, "Do you need healing in your lower back?"

She looked surprised, saying, "I do, actually. How did you know that?"

I replied, "Jesus loves you, and He shared that with me because He wants to heal you."

Her next words shook me. She said, "God really sees me?"

This one question communicates the purpose of words of knowledge. There is a world filled with people who want to feel *known*. They long to know that they are seen, loved, and cared for by God.

I proceeded to pray for her. As I did, God was faithful to heal her back.

She then said, "I've heard of God healing people before, and I never doubted it. I always believed. But this is the first time in my life where I understand that God loves me enough to do it for me…"

What would it look like if we learned to step out in faith with Jesus? What would it look like if we learned to follow the leading of Holy Spirit? Who could be impacted? Perhaps you've felt, at times, like my fifteen-year-old friend who desired to be used by God. Are you restless to live in purpose? Are you longing to be a bridge for the Father's love to impact hearts and lives?

Perhaps the fire stirring in your heart is Holy Spirit's invitation into adventure. Perhaps it's time to take a leap of faith.

*The wisdom of man is not sufficient.
We need the wisdom of God.*

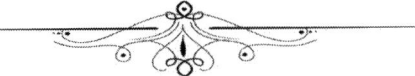

Chapter Seven
Messages of Wisdom

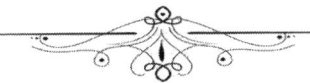

Throughout my years of travelling and speaking, I've met my fair share of leaders. I've met men and women—world leaders—who build with excellence, impacting the masses. While many of these leaders are remarkably intelligent, seasoned, and experts in their fields, there isn't a single one who is wise enough to lean on their own understanding. There isn't one who is capable of excelling apart from divine guidance. This tells me one thing: man's wisdom is not enough. We need the wisdom of God.

There is hardly anyone who understood this better than King Solomon.

The story of Solomon stepping into his kingship after his father, David's, death is in 1 Kings 3. Upon taking up the mantle of king, Solomon had a dream where God asked him, "Ask! What shall I give you?"

Solomon replied, "Now, O Lord my God, You have made Your servant king instead of my father David, but I am a little child; I do not know how to go out or come in. And Your servant is in the midst of Your people whom You have chosen, a great people, too numerous to be numbered or counted. Therefore give to Your servant an understanding heart to judge Your people, that I may discern between good and evil. For who is able to judge this great people of Yours?" (1 Kings 3:7-9).

In humility, Solomon asked for an understanding heart. He asked for wisdom. This wisdom would be something he would be renowned for amongst nations. From this point on, Solomon had a decision to make: Would he trust God's wisdom or his own?

While 1 Kings shares many examples of Solomon following the wisdom of God, we can see a scenario when he gave in to the wisdom of man.

1 Kings 11:1-3: "But King Solomon loved many foreign women, as well as the daughter of Pharaoh: women of the Moabites, Ammonites, Edomites, Sidonians, and Hittites—from the nations of whom the Lord had said to the children of Israel, 'You shall not intermarry with them, nor they with you. Surely they will turn away your hearts after their gods.' Solomon clung to these in love. And he had seven hundred wives, princesses, and three hundred concubines; and his wives turned away his heart."

Why was it that Solomon had so many wives? Firstly, we can see that he "loved" these women. Secondly, I have a theory that Solomon was operating in human wisdom rather than God's. I say this because Solomon didn't marry just anyone; he married princesses. It was likely that Solomon married women of nobility to create political alliances for Israel. We can see that it was these very women who turned Solomon's heart from the one true God. This was the fruit of following the wisdom of man rather than the wisdom of God.

Messages of wisdom differ from the other revelatory gifts. If we were to build a house, we could say that *prophecy* would show us what the house looks like in completion. *Knowledge* gives us the skills to create a thorough blueprint and to use the tools required. *Wisdom* helps us to navigate any rising issues during the building process.

A message of wisdom could be described as this: if someone is caught in a difficult circumstance that is beyond their human understanding to fix, a message of wisdom from God unlocks the problem.

I'll give you an example.

A few years ago, a business leader reached out to me, asking if he could schedule a phone call with me. He was looking for insight regarding a business decision. After consulting with the Lord, I felt peace about talking with him. Leading up to our conversation, the Lord spoke to me, saying, "He was just offered a prestigious job; however, the company is trying to severely underpay him."

I took the call.

This businessman began, saying, "I have a problem, and I think I need the word of the Lord. I was offered my dream job, but the company is trying to underpay me."

There is something to take note of here. As experienced as this man was in business, his wisdom and experience weren't enough. He needed wisdom from God.

While chatting with him, the Lord spoke to me, saying, "Tell him to turn down the opportunity and to begin negotiations from scratch."

I knew this would be a staggering leap of faith for him. As I communicated with him, the Lord began speaking to me about how he was to negotiate. I've done a bit of business here and there; however, I haven't done anything to the caliber that this man has. As I shared with him a strategy on how to negotiate his salary, I was astonished by my own words. I spoke wisdom that I know wasn't my own.

By the end of the phone call, he concluded that he was going to turn down the initial opportunity, suggesting starting negotiations from scratch.

One week later, he called me. Doing as I had instructed, he walked through the negotiation process, following the guidelines I set out for him. By the end of the week, the company gave him a new offer, doubling his annual income!

This was the fruit of a message of wisdom. This man had a dire circumstance that was beyond his control and understanding; therefore, God's wisdom came and unlocked his problem.

Proverbs 3:5-6: "Trust in the Lord with all your heart, and lean not on your own understanding; in all your ways acknowledge Him, and He shall direct your paths."

Messages of Wisdom Protocol

Moses operated proficiently in messages of wisdom. Exodus 18:13 says that Moses would sit from morning until evening as Israelites would approach him. They would list out their problems to him, and he would receive insight from the Lord.

If you are a highly pastoral person, then this might sound familiar. We often attribute the revelatory gifts in 1 Corinthians 12:4-11 to people who are primarily prophetic. Just as words of knowledge are often a primary gift for those who are highly evangelistic, messages of wisdom are essential to those with pastoral gifts. Highly pastoral people sometimes walk in high levels of messages of wisdom without even realizing it. When a pastoral person is ministering to someone, they might find themselves giving Holy Spirit-led advice to bring alignment to lives, breakthrough to circumstances, and healing to hearts.

Messages of wisdom will, at times, come across as Spirit-led direction. In saying this, I need to set up the proper parameters. I wouldn't recommend making a habit of giving directional prophetic words if you aren't seasoned in the prophetic ministry. When I say "seasoned," I'm not referring to those who have given a few prophetic words here or there. I'm referring to those who have allowed God to tune their ears to hear His voice and, therefore, are trusted by reputable leaders in their ability to hear the Lord.

If God entrusts you with a message of wisdom that is directional, I find it wise to approach it with humility. Vocabulary such as, "I feel that the Lord is saying…" is always a great approach, instead of saying definitively, "This is what God said for you to do." Remember that you are giving insight for someone else's life; therefore, they are the ones who feel the negative impact if you are wrong.

Another component to navigating messages of wisdom is discerning the timing of when to communicate. Here is a key that I believe every prophetic individual ought to know: It isn't our job to *say* everything we *see*. In all honesty, as a prophetic person, I probably only vocalize about ten percent of what I see and hear from God. I do this because I not only want my ears tuned to hear, but I also need to allow my tongue to become refined to speak in season.

Matthew 7:6: "Do not give what is holy to the dogs; nor cast your pearls before swine, lest they trample them under their feet, and turn and tear you in pieces."

Don't cast pearls before swine—what an important revelation. We need to submit to the timing of the Lord when it comes to revealing wisdom. Even though something might be clear to us, that doesn't necessarily mean God has commissioned us to be the one to bring order. We might think to ourselves, "If I know how to fix a problem, then why wouldn't I share?" We need to submit to the leading of the Lord. We can't go about casting wisdom everywhere with no restraint. Moses is a great example of this. Moses was a man who understood God's heart in wanting to free the Israelites. He understood God's wisdom in knowing that Israel couldn't be in captivity any longer; they needed to become great amongst nations.

One day, while walking in the desert, Moses saw an Egyptian fighting an Israelite. Out of a love and desire to see Israel free from slavery, he struck the Egyptian dead (Exodus 2:11-12). This act of passion resulted in tribulation for Moses with his own people. In fact, he needed to flee the land. God had already placed in Moses' heart the burden that He wanted to deliver the Israelites, but Moses tried to start the revolution of Exodus before its ordained time. Moses operated in wisdom in the wrong season. There is a time and place for when to act on what God has revealed to us. We can see the contrast of success forty years later when Moses contended for Israel's freedom at the proper time. If we are not able to guard God's word properly, not only does the message face unnecessary persecution, but so does the messenger.

The second reason why we shouldn't cast pearls before swine is because pearls are *round;* therefore, people may slip on them. Depending on someone's level of maturity, what is wisdom to us could be a stumbling block to someone else. The story of Jesus healing a leper gives a clear example of this:

Mark 1:42-45: "As soon as [Jesus] had spoken, immediately the leprosy left him, and he was cleansed. And He strictly warned him and sent him away at once, and said to him, 'See that you say nothing to anyone, but go your way, show yourself to the priest, and offer for your cleansing those things which Moses commanded, as a testimony to them.' However, he went out and began to proclaim it freely, and to spread the matter, so that Jesus could no longer openly enter the city, but was outside in deserted places; and they came to Him from every direction."

When Jesus cleansed the man from leprosy, the former leper had a newfound revelation of Christ. Discerning that the people's hearts in the city weren't yet ripe enough to receive Him, Jesus commanded the man to remain silent. Instead of obeying Jesus, the former leper's excitement drove him to speak freely of what had happened to him. Although this man's intent was to spread awareness of Jesus, the knowledge of the miracle closed the door for Jesus to have any platform in the city. Instead, He was banned outside in deserted places, lessening His potential to minister to a greater mass of people. We see here that truth spoken in the wrong season closed the hearts of the people.

Often, when I'm invited as a guest to speak at a church, God won't only tell me what to share; He also reveals to me what truths and testimonies to keep hidden. This isn't because God doesn't want that particular church to walk in the same revelation and wisdom He's given me. It's likely because they aren't yet ready to receive that specific truth in their hearts; they are in a different place in their walk with the Lord.

Here's an example: say that I was to go to a church that was just beginning to learn about hearing God's voice. In this scenario, I wouldn't come full force and share, say, my wildest stories about angelic encounters. My testimonies, which are precious to God's heart, could become a stumbling block. My job as a leader is to discern where the people are currently at so that I can serve them as best I can. I would probably come teaching, sharing the basics of how God can speak through the still, small voice and through visions. I would then slowly introduce them to the more mystical side of prophecy.

We need to be mindful of people's seasons, understanding that they are on a journey. There is a time to share wisdom; however, we need to come under the counsel of Holy Spirit to know when the appropriate time is to share God's message.

Let's flip the script for a moment. We've talked about giving messages of wisdom, but what if you are the recipient of a message from someone else? What if it's someone else speaking to you, giving direction? If someone is giving you a message of wisdom, here are some practical boundaries for you to practice before applying the word.

- Ask Holy Spirit.

Remember that you hear from God. We are not called to become co-dependent on others to hear Holy Spirit for us. Bounce the word off of Him, testing it with your discernment.

- Discern the fruit of the messenger.

I am an advocate for prioritizing proven character. I believe our character should always outweigh our gifting. That said, if I can't trust the fruit of the messenger, then I have the right to reject the message.

- Are there any manipulative motives behind the word?

Every expression of an individual's spirit has to come through the filter of their soul. If someone is wounded in heart and has not had proper prophetic training, they may try giving direction from a place of hurt.

An example would be, say, if someone said to you that God told them that you are supposed to give them finances. This would be a form of a manipulative directional word. God's word always honours free will. Words such as this should be disregarded.

- If you receive a directional word from someone and you are unsure of its validity, bring the word to trusted leadership in your life.

- If you are unsure of a directional word's validity, wait to see if God confirms the word through other trusted sources.

My wife and I have found it beneficial to have Spirit-led, trusted friends and leaders to speak into our lives. We have had many experiences when God has spoken to others, giving them messages of wisdom for us. These words have, at times, unlocked tremendous blessing in our lives.

You might be reading this right now, recognizing your need for God's wisdom in your life. Perhaps you are thinking about your relationships. Maybe you've felt stuck for years in endless cycles of drama. Perhaps you need breakthrough in your finances, feeling as though you have holes in your pockets. Maybe you feel visionless, as though you are continually waiting for strategy that never seems to come. What I know for certain is this: your wisdom isn't enough. The good news is that God's wisdom is at hand for you.

What would it look like if we learned to truly access God's wisdom? What if we could raise our families by God's leading? What if we made career or ministry decisions not by our own understanding but by the Lord's? Not only would we flourish in every area of life, but we would become a sign and wonder to everyone around us, pointing them to the goodness of God.

Child of God, you've been given the mind of Christ. Now isn't a time to lean on your own understanding; it is time to renew your heart, mind, and life in God's wisdom.

Dr. Luc Niebergall

Prayer

Pray this with me:

"Lord, thank You for giving me the mind of Christ. I pray for a heart of understanding. I ask You for wisdom. I realize that I cannot depend on this wisdom of this world. I cannot lean on my own understanding. I need Your wisdom, God. I ask You for the Spirit of wisdom and revelation. Help me to be wise in all my ways. Help me to be a sign and wonder, pointing people to the goodness of God.

"Amen."

Discerning of spirits is for discerning angels, demons, people, atmospheres, and, most importantly, to discern what Holy Spirit is doing.

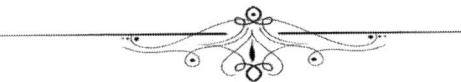

Chapter Eight
Discerning of Spirits

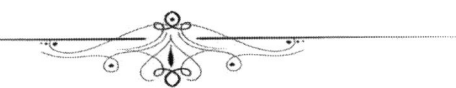

Discerning of spirits may be one of the most misunderstood gifts recorded in 1 Corinthians 12. While prophecy is an internalized gift—meaning that we hear Holy Spirit speaking from within—discerning of spirits is externally tapping into what is occurring around us.

People have often limited this gift to only discerning demonic spirits. One of the purposes for discerning of spirits is to discern demonic spirits that are tormenting people; however, this is only a fraction of the gift's purpose. This gift is not called "discerning of demonic spirits;" it is more general. This gift is also for discerning angelic spirits, people, and atmospheres and, most importantly, to discern what Holy Spirit is doing. When used healthily, this gift can become a safeguard, keeping us in the will of God for our lives.

Discerning the Spirit Realm

Ephesians 6:12: "For we do not wrestle against flesh and blood, but against principalities, against powers, against the rulers of the darkness of this age, against spiritual hosts of wickedness in the heavenly places."

We would be wise to remember that there is a spiritual war taking place around us. Discerning the spirit realm can consist of discerning angels and demons. We've already talked about angels in a previous chapter, so let's look more at discerning the *demonic*.

First, we need to ask ourselves the question: Why would we want to discern demons? It's simple. It's all about seeing people be set free.

When Jesus walked the earth, there were many manifestations seen throughout His ministry that were also seen in the Old Testament. Needless to say, Jesus did these things bigger and better than His predecessors. Jesus walked in healing and resurrection power, just like Elijah and Elisha. Profound teachings emerged through Jesus' ministry, just as Ezra and the Levites taught the Israelites about the Law (Nehemiah 8:6-8). Jesus came to shepherd a nation, just as David had. He had a signs-and-wonders ministry, just as Moses had.

There was one manifestation in His public ministry that made Him distinctly different than the men and women who went before Him. Jesus had the authority to command demons to flee. There is no record of demons fleeing upon someone's command in the Old Testament. The closest thing that I can find was when David would play his harp before King Saul, and it would bring him deliverance from his torment (1 Samuel 16:23). However, as far as demons fleeing upon someone's command, Jesus was the first.

Mark 1:27: "Then they were all amazed, so that they questioned among themselves, saying, 'What is this? What new doctrine is this? For with authority He commands even the unclean spirits, and they obey Him.'"

How, then, do we discern what is taking place around us for the purpose of seeing people set free? In my experience, people with gifts of discerning of spirits will either function as *seers* or *feelers*. We've already talked at length about seeing and vision, so let's focus more on the *feeling* side of discernment.

Discerning of spirits can often work similarly to words of knowledge. I'll paint a scenario for you:

Say that you are on your way to a gathering of people. You are feeling well emotionally and spiritually. The moment you step into the room, a thought about self-harm pops into your head. You don't normally think these thoughts, so you shrug it off without giving it further thought. However, what if this wasn't just a random thought? Perhaps you were discerning that someone in the gathering is being tormented by a spirit of "self-harm."

When I first began moving in discerning of spirits, I would walk into a place like, say, a coffee shop and would immediately feel overwhelmed. I would be swarmed by a bombardment of emotions because I was unknowingly feeling what others were experiencing in their lives. I would get around someone who wrestled with depression, and I would immediately begin to feel sluggish. I would leave feeling down and confused, when really it was my gift of discernment in operation. As a discerning person, I needed to learn to distinguish other people's state from my own reality. The truth is that these *feeling* senses are often a gift of discernment in its beginning stages.

In these types of scenarios, discerning of spirits has two steps. First, we discern what is occurring externally. Second, we discern internally what Holy Spirit is saying about it. We need to remember to function in the gifts in relationship with God. It is crucial to discern what Holy Spirit is saying.

I've met many people who move in this type of gifting and feel burdened when they discern. They feel as though they have spiritual insight and information yet don't understand the practical application. In truth, not everything we discern is our responsibility to deal with. If it were, then spiritually discerning people would burn out very quickly. Sometimes, we discern because Holy Spirit wants to give insight into how we can bring change and freedom to an individual. Perhaps we are supposed to minister to them, pray for them, or intercede on their behalf. Other times, we discern simply because we are discerning. Our responsibility is to be in communication with Holy Spirit and to keep in step with what He is doing and saying. We move when He moves; we are still when He is still.

It's important to address *prophetic delivery* when it comes to discerning the demonic. In training people to hear God's voice, I've discovered that those who are discerning can often wrestle with healthy prophetic delivery. The struggle comes because they will often *see* or *feel* what is occurring in the spirit realm, which can be difficult to translate into words.

Perhaps you've experienced words being spoken, such as, "You have a *spirit of confusion* over you, and God wants to deliver you from it." Even if the person truly did discern this, I believe that this is an improper way to share what is being discerned. I'll explain why:

In this scenario, the goal of the discerner would have been to bring awareness for the purpose of seeing the person set free. Here's the catch: if we tell someone that there is a demon tormenting them, it really doesn't matter what we say afterwards. I could follow this with the most encouraging prophetic word, but they won't hear it because I just played a role in fixing their eyes on the demonic. I likely struck fear in their heart. My goal was to see them set free, but I've actually just put them in more bondage.

When we discern demonic torment in someone's life, we can do what I call "flipping a word." Instead of pointing people to darkness, we can prophesy from the standpoint of victory. We are seated in heavenly places in Christ (Ephesians 2:6); therefore, we can see from the perspective of how the Father sees. We can prophesy blessing rather than magnifying the curse!

I'll give you an example of how we can healthily use our discernment to see someone set free:

Say I'm at a church service, and I see someone worshipping. Perhaps I either 'see' or 'feel' a spirit of confusion on their life.

My first step is to ask Holy Spirit, "Is there something you want me to do with what I'm discerning?"

If I feel like God says that He wants me to minister to them, I would approach by His leading. I wouldn't say to them, "You have a spirit of confusion tormenting you, and God wants to deliver you." I would instead say something like, "God is bringing you into a season of *clarity*. Things that haven't made sense will now be clear." Then I may add, "If there was any confusion, then God is removing that right now."

Since I am postured to see things from the Father's perspective, I can prophesy the opposite of what I'm discerning. If I see a spirit of confusion, I can prophesy clarity. If I see a spirit of anger, I can prophesy joy. If I see a spirit of anxiety, I can prophesy peace. Prophesying life dethrones death. Declaring light abolishes the darkness. This way, we aren't pointing to the enemy; we are directing people into God's will for their lives, resulting in freedom.

Discerning People

What does it mean to discern *people*?

I believe there are a few aspects to this. First of all, we can discern their *spirit*.

1 Samuel 9:19: "Samuel answered Saul and said, 'I am the seer. Go up before me to the high place, for you shall eat with me today; and tomorrow I will let you go and will tell you all that is in your heart.'"

Have you ever looked at someone and, without talking to them, you could immediately tell that they carried themselves with gentleness? We could chalk this up to being able to read people well, but what if it's more than that? The fruits of the Spirit (Galatians 5:22-23) can be shaped within us. What if you were discerning the fruit of gentleness in their life? Or, have you noticed that when a leader walks in the room, everyone takes notice? Many leaders tend to carry themselves a certain way. Eyes are drawn to them. Not only that, but their anointing is palpable. This could very well be us discerning their spirit.

Many years ago, I was window shopping in a mall. I was meandering around, not thinking about anything spiritual per se. At this time in my life, there was a specific minister I looked up to who lived abroad. Although I'd never met him, I had followed his ministry for a few years. I had grown accustomed to feeling the anointing that this man carried.

While wandering through the mall, I suddenly felt this man's anointing. The very same presence that I grew to discern while listening to his teachings was all of a sudden in the mall.

I said to the Lord, "God, I think he's in the mall right now."

In my natural understanding, I didn't even know if this man was in the country, let alone in the building. I made my way through the mall. To my surprise, there he was, buying ice cream with his wife! Through the gift of discerning of spirits, God granted me the gift of getting to meet and have a conversation with one of my role models in the faith. I now have the honour of calling him a *spiritual father* in my life.

I'm going to give you a quick exercise concerning discerning people:

Next time you are around a group of people, pay attention to what you sense on their lives. It is in our spirit that we carry the gifts and fruits of the Spirit. Our callings, anointings, and mantles abide in our spirit.

How does it feel being around someone whose ministry is primarily geared towards prayer and intercession? Does it contrast in comparison to being around someone who has an anointing and calling to business? Does being around someone who is primarily gifted in the prophetic feel different than someone who is, say, gifted pastorally or in teaching?

We can refine our gift of discernment to feel, see, and sense people's callings, mantles, anointings, and gifts.

Discerning people can also be essential to how we navigate our relationships. In fact, our history in relationships can become an essential tool for discernment. Take a look at this:

Matthew 13:24-30: "Another parable He put forth to them, saying: 'The kingdom of heaven is like a man who sowed good seed in his field; but while men slept, his enemy came and sowed tares among the wheat and went his way. But when the grain had sprouted and produced a crop, then the tares also appeared. So the servants of the owner came and said to him, "Sir, did you not sow good seed in your field? How then does it have tares?" He said to them, "An enemy has done this." The servants said to him, "Do you want us then to go and gather them up?" But he said, "No, lest while you gather up the tares you also uproot the wheat with them. Let both grow together until the harvest, and at the time of harvest I will say to the reapers, 'First gather together the tares and bind them in bundles to burn them, but gather the wheat into my barn.' " ' "

This parable is very applicable to relationships. Let me ask you something: Have you ever wondered why Jesus allowed Judas to be part of His twelve disciples? I have a theory. The first reason why Jesus likely had Judas close was for *Judas'* sake. I don't doubt that Jesus wanted the best for Judas, that he would be redeemed and transformed. Second, I believe Judas was permitted to be around for the sake of the other disciples. The eleven remaining disciples would become apostles to oversee the early church. It was imperative for them to understand what a false apostle looked like. I believe observing Judas was a part of their training. The truth is that sometimes God will permit a tare so that we know the difference between a tare and wheat. He will permit a tare so that we learn to discern between the counterfeit and the authentic.

Not too long ago, I saw a vision of many people who had arrows stuck in their backs. The pain from these arrows made the people move slowly and sluggish.

The Father then spoke, saying, "These arrows symbolize betrayal in relationships. Betrayal can severely wound—it has many faces. Sometimes it's gossip, slander, jealousy, competition, rejection, or abandonment."

I then saw the Father walk up to the wounded. He would lead them to forgive those who had betrayed them. He would then pull out the arrow, and the wound would immediately heal. Instead of throwing the arrow away, He would then place it in the person's hand.

The Father then said, "I'm healing wounds from betrayal in relationships. I had the formerly wounded keep the arrow that once harmed them as a reminder. When you are willing to be healed from relational wounds, you receive increased discernment in relationships."

Healed wounds become weapons of wisdom and discernment. We need to walk in discernment and submission to God with our relationships. Peering into our history of relationships can actually be a tool for increased discernment.

Increasing Discernment

Jesus was brilliant in His discernment. He was the most discerning person to ever walk the earth.

Take a look at this story:

Mark 5:25-31: "Now a certain woman had a flow of blood for twelve years, and had suffered many things from many physicians. She had spent all that she had and was no better, but rather grew worse. When she heard about Jesus, she came behind Him in the crowd and touched His garment. For she said, 'If only I may touch His clothes, I shall be made well.' Immediately the fountain of her blood was dried up, and she felt in her body that she was healed of the affliction. And Jesus, immediately knowing in Himself that power had gone out of Him, turned around in the crowd and said, 'Who touched My clothes?' But His disciples said to Him, 'You see the multitude thronging You, and You say, "Who touched Me?" ' "

In this scenario, Jesus is physically in a mob of people, shoulder to shoulder. One woman touches the hem of His garment, and He feels power go out from Him. Jesus was so tuned in to what was happening in the spirit realm that He noticed when a woman took power from Him by faith. His spiritual senses were so developed that even though

He was crammed in a group of people, He noticed the slightest shift in the atmosphere around Him. This shows us that what was in the spirit was just as real to Him as what was in the natural. This story, again, confirms to us that we've barely scratched the surface of understanding.

How, then, do we increase our discernment?

In recent years, I've stumbled upon what I consider to be a remarkable key concerning discernment. This key is found in Jesus' famous Sermon on the Mount.

Matthew 7:3-5: "And why do you look at the speck in your brother's eye, but do not consider the plank in your own eye? Or how can you say to your brother, 'Let me remove the speck from your eye'; and look, a plank is in your own eye? Hypocrite! First remove the plank from your own eye, and then you will see clearly to remove the speck from your brother's eye."

The key to discernment is found when Jesus says, "First remove the plank from your own eye, and then you will see clearly..." This poses the question: What are our planks, and are they preventing us from *seeing?*

Several years ago, there was a political shift happening in a nation. Prophetic words were running rampant regarding who would be the next person to rise into leadership. Many prophesied that one man in particular would step into office. During this time, I had a dream.

I won't share the details of this dream. However, in the dream, the Lord came to me, telling me who would win the election and why. I woke up from the dream and shared it with my wife. We were both confounded by the fact that it was the opposite candidate of who everyone else was prophesying would win. The Lord didn't permit me to share the dream other than with a few select people.

Although He often shares details with me concerning politics, He rarely permits me to share about it publicly.

The election came and went. The man who I dreamt would win won. The church, however, was left with a jarring question: Why were many of the prophetic words inaccurate?

It's important to ask these questions. In the prophetic community, we had missed the mark. Either we can pretend that this never happened, or we can ask the tough questions. The former leaves us to repeat the same mistakes. The latter thrusts us into greater maturity. For myself, I'm choosing the latter. I want to learn continually, even if it means admitting our wrongs.

So, then, where did we miss the mark in the prophetic community? I've come to believe that it's because some tried to interpret seasons and times through their own understanding and desires. The cultural act of blending religion and politics caused a distinct *plank*. This plank prevented people from being able to *see*.

While I just shared an example of a *cultural plank*, there are several different types of planks that we can have. Say that someone comes to one of my gatherings where I'm teaching about hearing God's voice. Perhaps this person grew up very conservatively, hearing teachings against the prophetic ministry. Even if I'm teaching straight from the Bible, they might not agree with a word I say because they are perceiving my words through a plank of false doctrine.

Another example could be if we held unforgiveness in our heart towards someone. Doing so would cause us to no doubt see them through the lens of bitterness. We would be incapable of seeing them as God sees them because we are holding offence in our heart. This offence creates a plank, hindering us from seeing them clearly.

Ephesians 1:18 (NIV): "I [Paul] pray that the eyes of your heart may be enlightened in order that you may know the hope to which he has called you, the riches of his glorious inheritance in his holy people."

Paul prays that the eyes of our hearts would be enlightened, showing that we see through the lens of our heart. There can be cultural planks, doctrinal planks, planks of offence, bitterness, or hurt. We could have planks of trauma. All of these planks are determined by what we have allowed to be established in our heart. Essentially, the healthier we allow our heart to become, the clearer we will see.

Matthew 5:8: "Blessed are the pure in heart, for they shall see God."

I don't desire to only discern angels or demons. I don't want to only discern people or atmospheres. I want to be able to tap into the greatest part of the gift of discernment: discerning what Holy Spirit is doing. It doesn't matter where I am, who I'm with, or what I'm facing; I want to be in tune with what Holy Spirit is doing.

We can't afford to have planks in our eyes. We need to foster purity of heart so that we can continually see God.

Dr. Luc Niebergall

Increasing Discernment Exercise

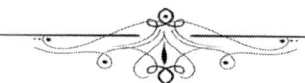

Here are some steps to take in order to partner with God in removing planks from our eyes, thus increasing our discernment:

1. Find a quiet place with the Lord.
2. Through speaking or writing ask God these questions:
   - *"Lord, do I have any planks of unforgiveness or offense?"*
   - *"Lord, do I have any planks of trauma or pain?"*
   - *"Lord, do I have any planks of fear?"*
   - *"Lord, do I have any cultural planks?"*
   - *"Lord, do I have any planks of false doctrine?"*
   - *"Lord, do I have any financial planks?"*
   - *"Lord, do I have relational planks?"*
3. With what the Lord has shown you, spend time praying through these planks, asking the Lord to heal and restore. God desires to remove planks. In return, you will have eyes to see.

PART III
Prophetic Lifestyle

God desires for healthy hearts to wield weighty gifts.

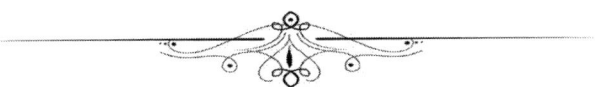

Chapter Nine
Prophetic Pitfalls

I am an adamant student of God's Word. I love the Bible, and not a day goes by without me being thankful that the Lord gave us such a wonderful gift to understand His heart. Something that I enjoy doing is looking through Scripture in search of the radical examples of God's goodness and power. Why do I do this, you ask? I do this because what I can see through the eyes of faith, I can believe for my own life.

So, then, what about prophecy? What extreme examples can we look at that can build our faith for hearing the voice of God? One of my favourite examples is of the two witnesses written about in the book of Revelation. Take a look at this:

Revelation 11:3: "And I [the Lord] will give power to my two witnesses, and they will prophesy one thousand two hundred and sixty days, clothed in sackcloth."

You may have theories about the two witnesses mentioned in this passage. I certainly have my own; however, this isn't a book on eschatology. What I want to note here is that these two witnesses will prophesy for one thousand two hundred and sixty days. Most of us likely struggle prophesying for three minutes! All jokes aside, there is a potent revelation here: the two witnesses graduated from the place of knowing how to prophesy to understanding how to live out the prophetic lifestyle. They knew how to rest in the spoken word of God.

In the church, we are shifting from a place of knowing how to hear the voice of God to living *from* His voice. This poses the question: How do we shift from giving prophetic words to living a prophetic lifestyle?

A prophetic lifestyle has less to do with gift activation than it has to do with posturing our lives properly. This is why I want to discuss the concept of *prophetic pitfalls*.

Since I have much experience training people in the prophetic ministry, I have become quite familiar with understanding the pitfalls that can follow highly prophetic people. These pitfalls are the very things that can hinder one from experiencing a true and healthy prophetic lifestyle. Throughout this chapter, I want to journey with you through some of the different pitfalls of the prophetic ministry.

Dismissing the Practical

Before I was in full-time ministry, I thought that in order to have a legitimate ministry, all I would need to do was know how to teach well, know how to prophesy accurately, and have enough faith to see the sick healed. When I did finally start up my ministry, I was blown away by the practicality required to run a ministry with excellence. I quickly began to understand that even if I can move in the gifts of the Spirit, if I do not also have a focus on administration, then I will not be able to impact as many people as I would like with said gifts.

Highly prophetic people have the tendency of excelling in things that are spiritual. Since there is such a grace to tap into things of the Spirit, there can often be a lack of understanding concerning the importance of practicality. This will often result in individuals being tremendously gifted yet having very noticeable holes in their life skills.

There is a side to moving in the Spirit that is completely supernatural; however, there is another side that is distinctly practical. I need to know how to prophesy, as well as how to keep on top of bookings for speaking engagements. I need to know how to pray for the sick, as well as how to have good people skills to effectively interact with other leaders. The truth is that if I weren't willing to continually grow in my faith for the supernatural—as well as in my life skills—it would give the enemy a foothold to negatively affect the impact I'm called to have.

It is not false humility to acknowledge our weaknesses or areas where we need growth. In fact, we are called to boast in our weaknesses. For myself, I've found tremendous value in acknowledging that one of my weaknesses in my earlier years was practicality. This is not everyone's weakness; however, it isn't something I naturally excelled in. In recognizing this with myself, I had the opportunity to surround myself with many amazing people who could coach me in more practical ways. I also surrounded myself with various business leaders who could offer counsel and insight as to how I should run the practical side of my ministry. Just because practicality is not an area that I naturally thrive in, this cannot be used as an excuse for me not to allow God to develop my practical life skills.

Whether it is our health, finances, relationships, or any other aspect of life, we need to discern how the supernatural and practical can be bound together. I would go as far as to say that in order to walk in maturity as a spiritual person, we need to be a place where both the supernatural and the practical marry.

The Tyranny of Assumption

Something I have often observed while working with different prophetic communities is that many will tend to slip into the *tyranny of assumption*. What I mean by this is that those who are highly prophetic can make a habit of trusting their discernment more than they put trust in proven relationships.

I will paint a picture for you:

Say that you've developed a close relationship with someone. They have proven themselves over time. One day at church, you see them. While crossing paths, it almost seems as though they are attempting to avoid eye contact with you. This is highly unlike them. You are now finding yourself confused by their actions. Soon, you find yourself frantically searching through your memory, trying to see if you can think of what you may have done to offend them. You feel your confusion about the situation evolving into frustration. This leads your mind to begin assuming what they are feeling towards you. Being a prophetic person, you may assume this is your discernment when really it's an assumption.

We can tread down a scary road when assumption is in control of the wheel. A healthy prophetic community requires training in kingdom relationships. Otherwise, we could begin trusting our "gift" more than our ability to have healthy communication in relationships.

Often, when we are in a stressful situation, such as experiencing conflict in a relationship, our emotions can cloud discernment. If we are only depending on our discernment, then in the name of "discernment," we can easily begin building a case against someone. We could create unnecessary distance with them simply because we are not willing to engage in healthy communication. This could even result in us talking badly about this person to others, inching into the territory of gossip and slander. This isn't to say that discernment isn't used in relationships—it absolutely is. We need to, however, allow the Lord to develop our relational skills as well as our spiritual gifts.

Probably some of the best advice I can give an emerging leader is this: revival is messy. Walking in relationships with people is messy. Instead of assuming others' faults and complaining about the mess, we need to learn how to grab a mop and clean it up. We need to learn how to do healthy communication and conflict in our relationships. Discernment and assumption are two different things entirely, so we cannot merge them. Discernment is when God gives us insight into a situation, whereas assumption is making an emotional analysis, which could easily be tainted by whatever is occurring within the realm of our soul.

It's in some of my most significant relationships where I've had many of my toughest conversations. It is a holy thing when friends can experience conflict yet assume the best of one another's hearts. Instead of casting each other aside, this allows us to healthily navigate offence, often resulting in greater connection.

Valuing Gifting Above Character

The importance of cultivating godly character is one of the topics I am most passionate about.

Jesus gave a descriptive teaching about this. He said, "You will know [false prophets] by their fruits. Do men gather grapes from thornbushes or figs from thistles? Even so, every good tree bears good fruit, but a bad tree bears bad fruit" (Matthew 7:16-17).

When Jesus said, "You will know them by their fruits," what type of fruit was He referring to? It could be debated that Jesus was talking about prophesying, healing the sick, etc., but that would contradict what He said a few verses later. He said, "Not everyone who says to Me, 'Lord, Lord,' shall enter the kingdom of heaven, but he who does the will of My Father in heaven. Many will say to Me in that day, 'Lord, Lord, have we not prophesied in Your name, cast out demons in Your name, and done many wonders in Your name?' And then I will declare to them, 'I never knew you; depart from Me, you who practice lawlessness!'" (Matthew 7:21-23).

I'll share a story with you:

A few years ago, I was ministering in the Caribbean to a group of youth. These youths were troubled. Some were drug addicts; others were in gangs. I don't think there was a single one of them who knew Jesus. They undeniably needed a touch from the love of God.

Receiving a word of knowledge, I said, "Who is it here who needs healing in their left ankle?"

The youth pastor put up his hand, confirming that it was him.

I looked to all of the unsaved youth, saying, "I want to show you all the power of Jesus' name."

Pointing to one of the youths, I said to him, "Put your hand on your pastor's ankle and say 'Jesus.' Watch what happens."

The boy reached down, reluctantly saying Jesus' name. As he did, the pastor felt the power of God, causing him to jump into the air. When he landed, his ankle was healed! We saw Jesus heal so many ailments, all from kids who didn't even know Jesus before that day.

Now, why did I share this story? I did so to show you that even non-believers can move in power. Why is that? It's because there is power in the name of Jesus. The healings we witnessed that day weren't fruit from these kids' lives; it was fruit from Jesus' name. Does this mean that someone can be gifted but not be trusted? Absolutely. Judas healed the sick and cast out demons, yet we all know how his story unfolded. What fruit are we looking for, then?

We are to look for the fruit that can only be shaped by truly knowing Jesus.

Galatians 5:22-23: "But the fruit of the Spirit is love, joy, peace, longsuffering, kindness, goodness, faithfulness, gentleness, self-control. Against such there is no law."

I've felt a poignant tension in my ministry throughout the years. It is easy to activate people in the gifts of the Spirit but impossible to activate them in the fruits. The fruits of the Spirit can only grow in one place: in friendship with God.

Scripture is clear on the importance of spiritual giftedness. We are commanded to eagerly desire it (1 Corinthians 14:1). That said, each of us carries the responsibility to make sure that our character outweighs our gifting. We need to make sure that our love outweighs our platform.

Isaiah 6 shares a story about the prophet Isaiah encountering God in the throne room. He witnesses angels—the seraphim. In this vision, one of these angels carries a coal from the altar, touching the prophet's lips. The angel then spoke, saying, "Behold, this has touched your lips; your iniquity is taken away, and your sin is purged" (Isaiah 6:7).

As a prophetic mouthpiece, Isaiah's lips needed to be refined. How, then, are we to allow our lips to be refined to speak the word of the Lord? I'll show you with a verse:

Matthew 12:34: "For out of the abundance of the heart the mouth speaks."

Refined lips require a refined heart. In other words, the weight of our words is determined by the health of our heart. God desires for healthy hearts to wield weighty gifts.

This might sound like an obscure statement, but when I'm looking to see if I can trust a leader, I don't look at how well they can prophesy. I look to see how they speak to their spouse. I'm looking to see if the fruit of gentleness is shaped in their life because I know it can only come from one place: encountering the Father's heart. I'm looking to see if they've allowed the fruit of joy to be shaped in them because it can only be grown by encountering Jesus, who is Joy.

Why do we need to put such an emphasis on character—the fruits of the Spirit? Why not chase *only* gifting? It's because we aren't called to burn for Jesus for only a season. We are meant to burn for Him for a lifetime.

You aren't called to only impact people with your gifts. You are also called to show generations that come after you what it looks like to live a life of purity, wholeness, and longevity. The only way to leave a legacy with your gift is with good enough character to sustain you for a lifetime.

Over-Spiritualism

In the past decade or so, there has been a vast amount of revelation being revealed in the church concerning prophetic experiences. God has been showing the church our accessibility to different experiences and encounters that men and women experienced in biblical times. These are things that we have entry to through the cross. Some of these encounters that God has been shining light on include transportation (Acts 8:26-40), angelic visitations

(Matthew 4:11), heavenly encounters (Isaiah 6, Ezekiel 1, Daniel 7), visitations from the Lord Himself (Acts 9:1-19), etc. Prophetic encounters are along the mystical side of the prophetic ministry. Many try to steer away from this vein of Christianity; however, it is important to remember that prophetic encounters are a pivotal tool to wholeness and Christlikeness, and are deeply scriptural.

One of the hurdles when the church receives new revelation is the temptation to pull it to unhealthy extremes. I am an advocate for prophetic experiences. I live a lifestyle of experiencing them. That said, we must remember that such things need to be sourced by love and stewarded with integrity. If we have a grace to see and hear the word of the Lord in mystical ways, yet we are not rooted in friendship with God and grounded in Scripture, there can often be a pull towards forms of over-spiritualism. Pursuing such experiences with a poor heart posture can open up many doors for deception, such as a worship of spiritual experiences and even New Age mentalities. If our heart posture is incorrect while desiring such encounters, we could end up being led by our own will rather than by Holy Spirit.

I'm very open to prophetic encounters. I want whatever the Lord desires for me. However, if Holy Spirit isn't in control of the wheel, then I don't want anything to do with it. We need to remember that a prophetic experience isn't the end goal; Jesus is the end goal—always. We shouldn't be in pursuit of encounters for the sake of experiencing the supernatural; we need to be in pursuit of encounters to know Jesus more.

Not only should we be consumed by a hunger to know the Lord, but we should also be entrenched in the written Word of God: the Bible. When pursuing prophetic encounters, relationship with Holy Spirit and being rooted in Scripture is what keeps us grounded in truth. I have witnessed many go off the deep end in what they perceive as truth because they see more validity in what they have felt prophetically, compared to what is written in Scripture. As a result, their doctrine is shaped, say, by ninety percent encounter and only ten percent Bible. The prophetic word will always submit to the written Word. The *rhema* submits to the *logos*. Every time. Every prophetic thing we experience may not be written in black and white in the Bible, but Scripture should always support what we experience. The prophetic should never contradict Scripture because God is not divided; He is constant and unchanging.

In the scriptural accounts of prophetic encounters, there was always a natural manifestation coming from such experiences. This means that we can test the validity of an encounter by the tangibility of its fruit. Ezekiel's heavenly encounter in Ezekiel 1 resulted in him stepping into his prophetic calling to bring change to Israel. Isaiah's encounter in the throne room of God in Isaiah 6 resulted in him being a prophetic voice to government. The apostle Paul's encounter, when Jesus came to him in Acts 9, launched him into becoming an apostle to the gentiles.

True encounters bear legitimate fruit. As we partake of Jesus in such ways, we should begin to look more like Him. We should be learning to love the way that He loves. If someone claims that they are having these types of encounters yet they are not radiating more love as a result, then I believe we have the right to question the legitimacy of the encounter.

Pride

Pride can be one of the more dangerous pitfalls for prophetic individuals. This pitfall doesn't only hurt the individual carrying pride, but it could very well end up wounding others. Prophetic individuals who harbour deep wounds of rejection can slip into mentalities of believing that they are always right and that everyone else is in error. This is where I have seen people use the prophetic ministry as a means to speak out against the church and church leadership. The prophetic ministry should never be used as a weapon against people; it should be used as a weapon against the enemy. This level of pride can, unfortunately, result in manipulation and control under the guise of a "prophetic gift."

Matthew 7:15-16: "Beware of false prophets, who come to you in sheep's clothing, but inwardly they are ravenous wolves. You will know them by their fruits."

The difference between true prophets and false prophets is that true prophets point to Jesus, whereas false prophets point to themselves. When I use the term "false prophet," I am not referring to someone who has given an incorrect prophetic word; we are all learning and growing in how we hear the Lord. I am referring to those who, out of pride, use their prophetic gift to intentionally manipulate and control others because they themselves are wounded.

I don't use the term "false prophet" often or lightly, and when I do, I am very careful in doing so. In fact, I have met very few whom I believe have walked in this level of deception. However, we need to be aware of the schemes of the enemy through false prophets. We also need to test our own hearts to make sure that we are ministering from a place of love instead of from soulish desires.

Conclusion

While reading through this chapter, the Lord may have highlighted specific things in your own heart. Perhaps you've observed pitfalls where you've unintentionally treaded. If this is the case, don't be disheartened. One of the amazing things about God is that He is eager to help us mature. He is quick to forgive and refine us. Remember that God loves you and desires for you to walk in a prophetic lifestyle where you are saturated by His voice and word.

While reading this chapter, if you noticed any area in your life where you need freedom, please pray this prayer with me:

"Holy Spirit, I pray for a revelation of friendship with You. I ask for face-to-face encounters and heart-to-heart moments with You. I choose to come closer. I repent for any pitfalls that I have either intentionally or unintentionally stepped into. Create in me a clean and healthy heart. Refine me. Heal me. Mature me. Teach me how to step into encountering a prophetic lifestyle. Teach me to be consumed by Your word.

"Amen."

The prophetic multiplies in prophetic community.

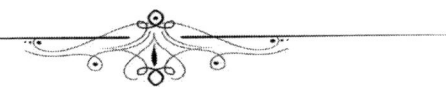

Chapter Ten
Prophetic Community

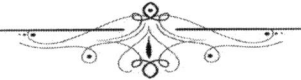

It was only several years ago when I found myself reading through 1 and 2 Samuel. I was reflecting on the life of David and how he was such a radical pursuer of the heart of God. I read about how he'd risen from impossible odds into kingship in Israel.

Inspired by the captivating story, the Lord spoke to me, saying, "Luc, I'm going to burst your bubble right now. You're not a *David*."

I was taken aback. I replied, "If I'm not a *David*, then what am I?"

He said, "Samuel anointed David as king of Israel. You're a Samuel, called to raise kings and queens. Samuel wasn't only a prophetic voice; he was a *father*."

My wife and I have had the honour of being surrounded by many young people whom we have the honour of fathering, mothering, and loving on. I used to favour speaking to the masses from stages; now, I favour sitting with sons and daughters around tables. Over the past several years, I've been in the process of picking up perhaps the greatest piece of my calling, which is to be a father to the fatherless.

One day, I'll write a book on fathering and mothering upcoming generations, but I'll save that for another time. What I want to focus on now is the correlation between community and the prophetic ministry. In fact, I believe that community and a revelation concerning the *family of God* is a distinct key to experiencing increase in the prophetic.

Increased Prophetic

How is it that we can see an increase in the prophetic? We can exercise our gift; this is crucial. We can receive from prophetic ministries. We can avoid prophetic pitfalls. There are a variety of different ways to experience increase. Recently, I stumbled upon a fascinating revelation in Scripture: the prophetic multiplies in prophetic community.

The Old Testament highlights the lives of a vast number of prophets. Israel was built, shaped, and guided by the words of prophets. That said, we only see two places where the prophetic *multiplies*.

The first place where we witness multiplication is with Saul and the concession of prophets.

1 Samuel 10:10-11: "When they came there to the hill, there was a group of prophets to meet [Saul]; then the Spirit of God came upon him, and he prophesied among them. And it happened, when all who knew him formerly saw that he indeed prophesied among the prophets, that the people said to one another, 'What is this that has come upon the son of Kish? Is Saul also among the prophets?'"

Here we see Saul rubbing shoulders with a prophetic community, and what happens? He begins to prophesy as though he were a prophet. We not only see a demonstration of prophecy; we see prophecy multiplying in community!

The second place we see the prophetic multiplying is in Elijah and Elisha's relationship.

2 Kings 2:9-13: "Elijah said to Elisha, 'Ask! What may I do for you, before I am taken away from you?' Elisha said, 'Please let a double portion of your spirit be upon me.' So he said, 'You have asked a hard thing. Nevertheless, if you see me when I am taken from you, it shall be so for you; but if not, it shall not be so.' Then it happened, as they continued on and talked, that suddenly a chariot of fire appeared with horses of fire, and separated the two of them; and Elijah went up by a whirlwind into heaven. And Elisha saw it, and he cried out, 'My father, my father, the chariot of Israel and its horsemen!' So he saw him no more. And he took hold of his clothes and tore them into two pieces. He also took up the mantle of Elijah that had fallen from him, and went back and stood by the bank of the Jordan."

Elijah was a fascinating prophet. By many, he is known as the *lone prophet* because of what he said while sitting under the broom tree:

1 Kings 19:9-10: "And there he went into a cave, and spent the night in that place; and behold, the word of the Lord came to him, and He said to him, 'What are you doing here, Elijah?' So he said, 'I have been very zealous for the Lord God of hosts; for the children of Israel have forsaken Your covenant, torn down Your altars, and killed Your prophets with the sword. I alone am left; and they seek to take my life.'"

In his lifetime, Elijah accomplished tremendous feats against the kingdom of darkness. His calling, however, wasn't only to be a prophet; it was also to be a father. He proved his success as a prophet when he called fire down from heaven and slayed the four hundred false prophets of Baal (1 Kings 18). He ultimately proved faithful in his calling as a father when his spiritual son didn't divert his eyes when he ascended to heaven (2 Kings 2:9-13).

As Elijah ascended, Elisha didn't call out, saying, "My mentor, my mentor!" He didn't call out, saying, "Prophet, prophet!" He said, "My father, my father!" These words reveal so much. They reveal that Elijah, the lone prophet, passed the test of *family*. Because of this, Elijah had the authority to see the prophetic that was on his life multiplied into the generation who would come after him. The prophetic multiplied in community and family.

Not only does the prophetic multiply within prophetic community but there is accountability in living out our prophetic destiny. As I've journeyed with several spiritual sons and daughters, I've not only been used as a voice to speak prophetically into their lives; I've also been used as a father to help launch them into fulfillment of their words.

With many of these sons and daughters, our relationship began with me prophesying destiny into their lives. These relationships then blossomed when I began journeying with them to see the words fulfilled. For many, I prophesied that they would speak to the masses, only then to train them in public speaking and putting together messages. For others, I've prophesied writing, then took them under my wing, resulting in them publishing books.

There isn't always such immediate practical application in seeing our words come to pass, but this poses a question. What would it look like if we had the kind of community where we related to one another based on how God sees us? What if we saw one another through the lens of prophetic destiny? I believe that this is exactly what David did.

Before David was the king of Israel, he first became the king of those who were rejected by Israel (1 Samuel 22:2). David took several men who were branded as rejects and turned them into his mighty men (2 Samuel 23:8-39); those known throughout the nation of Israel as men of valour (I Chronicles 12). David looked at these men, seeing past what the rest of Israel saw. He perceived them through the very eyes of God, thus having authority to catapult them into their God-given destinies. David received those who didn't feel as though they belonged; he fathered them and taught them to walk in greatness. The feats of war from these men even surpassed David's.

This is the power we carry. We can look into someone who does not even believe in themselves and call greatness out from them. We can choose to relate to them based on how God sees them. This is the power of prophetic community.

Overcoming Lone Ranger Mentalities

There is another pitfall in the prophetic ministry—one that I left out of the previous chapter in order to expound on how it relates to community. This pitfall is perhaps one of the most common for prophetic individuals. This pitfall is *isolation*.

You might be thinking, "Wait a minute—can't isolation be a good thing?" Moments of isolation can absolutely be good. God may even permit seasons of isolation. Jesus exemplified moments of isolation; He often withdrew to be with the Father. We should do the same—this is a part of fostering friendship with God. Jesus, however, never exemplified a *lifestyle* of isolation.

One of the reasons this is such a distinct pitfall is because of rejection that can come with the territory of the prophetic ministry. Prophetic individuals can experience rejection because of others' false narratives of prophecy. Unfortunately, in some circles, the prophetic ministry is deeply misunderstood. Throughout the years, I've met many who have been rejected due to how they hear the Lord. Thankfully, we are in a time where hearing God's voice is becoming quite widespread throughout the body of Christ. Even in many conservative churches, this concept is being embraced.

What do we do, then, if we experience this form of rejection? There are really only two responses. We can either pull rejection into our heart or we can bring it to the Father. If we pull rejection into our heart, then we will succumb to a rejection wound. This will often cause us to withdraw from people. It results in isolation. When we instead bring our hurts to the Father, we see that His acceptance is far greater than the world's rejection.

Time and time again, I have met prophetic people who, due to wounding, try to avoid being accountable in relationships. Often, prophetic people will interpret the freedom that the cross granted us as permitted autonomy from relational commitment. They can slip into a lie that assumes their gift works better apart from covering and accountability. Trying to operate as a prophetic person apart from community and accountability will lead down a long road of wounding. God doesn't want us to live as an island. He wants to graft us into community where we can thrive, be affirmed, and championed.

In John 17, Jesus prays His final recorded prayer and begins to talk to the Father about how He had been faithful with what was given to Him. It is interesting to me that Jesus doesn't mention the things that a lot of us would likely mention when talking about our successes.

Jesus didn't talk to the Father about how He was in spotlight ministry where the masses would follow Him day and night. He didn't mention His healing ministry or how, through His teaching ministry, He unveiled mysteries that had not been discovered since the foundations of the earth were made. He didn't mention His prophetic ministry. Instead, Jesus talked to the Father about how He was faithful with the twelve disciples who were given to Him. Even though Jesus was used as the catalyst that redirected history, He shows us that one of His main focuses and mandates was to be committed in relationship with those the Father had given Him.

If you are reading this and you have experienced rejection from the church because of your prophetic gift—as a leader in the church and on behalf of the church, I apologize to you. I declare over you that you are irreplaceable in the heart of God and valuable in His kingdom. There is a place in the family of God that fits who you are perfectly. I pray that Jesus surrounds you with those who will accept and love you. I pray that fathers and mothers of the faith will come around you to help steward and nurture the calling over your life.

You were not created to be alone. You were fashioned to know that you belong. Belonging can launch you where isolation cannot.

Well-roundedness is an essential key to prophetic lifestyle.

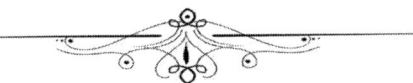

Chapter Eleven
Prophetic Leadership

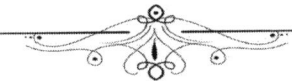

No matter who you are reading this book, you are called as a leader. Perhaps you're called as a leader in ministry or business. Or, maybe you are a leader in your community or in your home. Wherever we are called to lead, there is a proverb that we would be wise to remember: It's not enough to be a *leader;* we need to be a *healthy leader.*

I recall being in my mid-twenties. I had been travelling for a few years, training people to hear the voice of God. As young as I was, I had witnessed amazing things in these early years of ministry. I remember teaching seminars on the prophetic ministry. When people first came, many didn't even believe God wanted to speak to them. By the end of the classes, these very same students could give ten prophetic words one after another.

One day, I was making my way through the city, running errands. On three separate occasions throughout the day, I bumped into students who attended a seminar

I'd taught on hearing God's voice. I quickly realized that these interactions were a set-up from the Lord. There was something He wanted to teach me.

Conversing with each person, it was undeniable that they had grown in their ability to hear God through the classes. They knew how to prophesy; however, I noticed something else: they weren't rooted in the written Word of God. Not only that, but they didn't know how to take the prophetic and use it as a tool to reach those who didn't yet know Jesus. They wrestled in their relationships. They didn't have grand vision for their lives. That's when the realization struck me: I was no doubt training people in the prophetic ministry, but by not putting emphasis on other facets of God, I was also training them to be unbalanced.

This was the encouragement I needed to begin dreaming with God. My wife and I founded a ministry school called *Royal Identity Academy,* where we train and equip people in the things of God. We cover topics from friendship with God, heart health, and biblical literacy all the way to subjects such as prophecy, healing, and leadership. Our goal is to train people to be well-rounded in their relationship with God for the purpose of reaching their spheres of influence. I love hearing the amazing testimonies from our students of how God has used them to impact people around them. Our students see fruit not only because they are trained to hear; they are equipped to encounter all of the different facets of Jesus.

Well-roundedness is an essential key to prophetic lifestyle. How, then, do we cultivate it? A main component is learning to receive the full expression of Christ's leadership.

Ephesians 4:11-12: "And [Jesus] Himself gave some to be apostles, some prophets, some evangelists, and some pastors and teachers, for the equipping of the saints for the work of ministry, for the edifying of the body of Christ."

In many church circles, apostles, prophets, evangelists, pastors, and teachers are referred to as the *five-fold ministry*. Biblically, they are an expression of God's leadership. When Jesus walked the earth, He was the full embodiment of the five-fold ministry. Jesus was—and still is—our great Apostle, Prophet, Evangelist, Pastor, and Teacher. When He died, rose again, and ascended into heaven, in His wisdom, He scattered these five callings into different individuals. I believe His will is that they would function together in one body again, which is the body of Christ.

Although this isn't meant to be a thorough teaching on the five-fold ministry, for the sake of practicality, I will present a quick overview. This will give you a foundation as you continue reading.

Apostle - Apostles are visionaries who receive strategy of what it would look like for heaven to invade earth in a sustained move of God. They function as catalysts and builders to bridge their God-given vision into reality. Their job in the body of Christ is also to train the rest of the church to be apostolic-minded. They are to train the church to receive heaven's heart and vision for each individual's entrusted sphere of influence.

Prophet - Prophets have a supernatural grace over their lives to hear and speak the word of God. They will more than likely have the ears of very influential people to speak into, bringing prophetic direction and guidance. A prophet's job within the church is also to train and equip the rest of the church in how to hear and speak the word of the Lord. When this is achieved, every individual in the church becomes a vessel for God's word to be spoken through.

Evangelist - Evangelists have a deep burden for those who do not yet know Jesus. They are passion- and compassion-driven to see the gospel impacting beyond the four walls of the church. One of the primary functions of an evangelist is to train and equip the rest of the church in how to become evangelistic.

Pastor - Pastors have a passion for bringing healing to the broken-hearted; therefore, they carry a strong anointing to bring restoration to the wounded soul. Pastors also hold revelation of how to live out community and kingdom relationships. Pastors are gatherers and lead by doing life with people. A pastor's job within the church is to train and equip the rest of the church in how to become pastoral.

Teacher - Teachers have a grace over their lives to tap into revelatory truths from the written word of God. They have a great focus on teaching and studying so they can train the church to access deep truths within Scripture. Teachers function by guiding the church in how to live a Christ-like life through biblical teachings.

Not everyone is called to carry one of these five callings. In fact, I propose there may even be far fewer than we might assume. As stated in Ephesians 4:11-12, the five-fold ministry is to "equip the saints for the work of ministry." Not all of us carry the influence to train and equip the church. Most of us are called to different spheres of influence entirely.

Now, let's address the question you are likely thinking: Why is Luc talking about the five-fold ministry in a book on prophecy?

I'll tell you why. It's not enough to only know how to hear God. If we are to truly lead in our spheres of influence, we are going to have limited fruit if we only prophesy all day. We also need to know how to receive apostolic vision so that we can build! We need to have an evangelistic heart for those who don't know Jesus. We need to thrive pastorally in kingdom relationships. We need to be rooted in truth as a teacher would be. Each of us carries the responsibility to encounter Jesus as our Apostle, Prophet, Evangelist, Pastor, and Teacher. This is an essential key to wholeness. It is an essential key to healthy and effective leadership.

Several years ago, I was teaching at a small school on hearing the voice of God. For several weeks straight, we had about seventy students who were eagerly growing in the prophetic ministry. Leading up to the final week of the school, I announced to the students that for the final session, we were going to do something different: we were going out to a nearby train station to practice everything we had learned in class. We were going to give prophetic words to those who didn't yet know Jesus.

Being optimistic, I thought everyone would be thrilled! After all, what is the purpose of growing in spiritual gifts if we aren't reaching people through them? The final session finally came. Expecting the same turnout, I was astounded to witness our numbers dwindle from seventy people to seven!

As much as I would have loved to have had seventy people at the train station prophesying, we went out nonetheless. God used those seven brave warriors to impact a lot of lives that evening.

My wife and I laugh thinking back to this moment, finding it amusing; however, there is a significant truth evident in this story. Many people from this particular group were very comfortable with receiving from *Jesus the Prophet*. They were comfortable with learning how God speaks. They loved learning about visions and dreams. Yet, they felt uncomfortable with *Jesus the Evangelist*. Without even realizing it, they had compartmentalized how they received from Jesus.

We have a tendency to find comfort in the familiar. We will often unwittingly position ourselves to receive from leaders who have similar giftsets as us. As a result, we have the intuitive ones only receiving from prophets, or the tender-hearted ones only receiving from pastors. We have the studious receiving only from teachers, or those with missional mindsets only surrounding themselves with evangelists. We risk building upon partial truths. We would be wise to remember that when we compartmentalize how we are receiving from Jesus, we are making the decision to become unbalanced. We each bear the responsibility of allowing Jesus, our great Apostle, Prophet, Evangelist, Pastor, and Teacher, to take shape inside of us.

I don't only want aspects of Jesus; I want all of Him. I don't just want to lead; I want to lead well. This requires heart examination. Are we receiving from Jesus the Apostle? Are we allowing ourselves to truly be apostolic-minded to know how to build His kingdom in our spheres of influence? Are we renewing our minds in God's vision, dreams, and desires for our lives?

Are we receiving from Jesus the Prophet? Are we allowing ourselves to learn to hear the voice of God? Are we discerning our seasons and times with Him? Are we allowing ourselves to live by the words He speaks?

Are we receiving from Jesus the Evangelist? Are we allowing His heart for people to well up within us? Have we allowed Him to show us how He wants to use us to reach those who don't yet know Him?

Are we receiving from Jesus the Pastor? Have we invited Him in to heal the wounded areas of our souls? Have we allowed Him to train us in kingdom relationships?

Are we receiving from Jesus the Teacher? Have we allowed Him to root us in the written word of God? Have we allowed Him to use circumstances in our lives to teach us?

If you desire to experience Jesus in fullness, I invite you to pray this prayer with me:

"Jesus, thank You that You desire to encounter me in fullness. I repent for any time I may have compartmentalized how I've received You. I receive You as my Apostle. Train me to build Your kingdom on the earth. I receive You as my Prophet. Teach me to hear Your voice. I receive You as my Evangelist. Teach me how to burn like Your heart burns for those who don't yet know You. I receive You as my Pastor. Bring health to my heart and relationships. I receive You as my Teacher. Teach me to encounter You through Your written Word. Train me so I may be appropriately equipped to impact the sphere of influence to which You've called me."

A Deeper Look at Prophets

Since this is a book on hearing God's voice, let's talk specifically about *prophets* for a moment.

Throughout the years, my theology about prophets has ebbed, flowed, and ultimately matured. While I don't feel a current burden to write a thorough teaching on the office of a prophet, I do want to bring clarity concerning some elementary principles. There may, perhaps, be a day when the Lord releases me to write an in-depth teaching on the revelation I've received on the topic.

Often, due to a lack of definition, we tend to assume that prophetic people and prophets are the same thing when really they are distinctly different. Back in the 1980s, when there was a wave of restoration regarding the prophetic ministry, it was commonly believed that if you prophesied, you were a prophet. This resulted in many people proclaiming themselves as prophets and prophetesses of God. While Scripture tells us that every believer can prophesy, not everyone who prophesies is a prophet. We can see in the Old Testament that there were many people who prophesied yet were not prophets. King Saul was an example of this.

In 1 Samuel 10, Saul encountered a concession of prophets. Since he was with them, he began to prophesy alongside them. It is important to note that even though Saul prophesied, he is not scripturally referred to as a prophet. This shows us that there is much more responsibility required in being a prophet than simply prophesying. We are all called to prophesy; however, to be a prophet is a very set-apart calling from the Lord.

We've previously discussed how prophetic people minister. "He who prophesies speaks edification and exhortation and comfort to men" (Corinthians 14:3). Let's compare that to how prophets minister.

Jeremiah 1:9-11: "Then the Lord put forth His hand and touched my [Jeremiah's] mouth, and the Lord said to me: 'Behold, I have put My words in your mouth. See, I have this day set you over the nations and over the kingdoms, to root out and to pull down, to destroy and to throw down, to build and to plant."

Prophetic people are mandated to prophesy to individuals. While prophets will do this as well, they are also mandated to be a voice to cities, regions, and nations. My standard has grown to be quite high for those considered to be prophets. One of my staple questions to gauge if someone is functioning in maturity as a true prophet is: Have they given a word that has changed a nation? Like I said—I've grown to have high standards.

When God called Samuel to anoint David as king, Samuel wasn't simply giving a confirming word that he would rise to monarchy. Samuel *anointed* him for kingship. This means that David wouldn't have become king if Samuel, as a prophet, hadn't anointed him. Samuel wasn't functioning in a prophetic gift; he was pronouncing the word of the Lord. This was the power that prophets carried in the Old Testament. Nations were moved, shaped, and built by their very words. Why would we expect anything less in present times? While the body of Christ functions in a prophetic gift, prophets wield the word of the Lord. These are two markedly different things.

Those who have the calling of a prophet are God-appointed and people-appointed, never self-appointed. They are God-appointed in the sense that prophets in the Bible were first and foremost called and risen by God. We can see this with how God first called the prophet Jeremiah.

Jeremiah 1:5: "Before I formed you in the womb I knew you; before you were born I sanctified you; I ordained you a prophet to the nations."

Prophets aren't only God-appointed; they are also people-appointed. If someone is a prophet, they shouldn't have to run around calling themselves one. In fact, as you live out the unique expression of the calling, leaders will begin to recognize the mantle over your life. Prophets are people-appointed in the sense that credible leaders should recognize the calling, without them having to self-identify.

Another marker is that prophets will train and equip the church to hear the voice of God. Remember, prophets are "for the equipping of the saints for the work of ministry" (Ephesians 4:11-12). Again, the prophet Samuel shows us an excellent example of a true prophet.

1 Samuel 3:1: "Now the boy Samuel ministered to the LORD before Eli. And the word of the LORD was rare in those days; there was no widespread revelation."

This verse states that the word of the Lord was rare in Israel during this time period. This lack reveals Samuel's mandate as a prophet. Samuel did far more than prophesy; he was a gift to Israel, mandated to make God's word common again. Not only did Samuel prophesy to common-day people, but he appointed kings by the direction of God. Samuel was a prophetic counsellor and advisor to both kings and priests. He even rose a concession of prophets (1 Samuel 10). In Samuel, God appointed one man who made the word of the Lord common throughout an entire nation. We can actually see the fruit of Samuel's ministry echoing throughout generations in 1 Kings and 2 Kings, in the vast number of prophets who existed throughout that time. These prophets were likely the fruit of Samuel's ability to train and equip others to walk in the prophetic ministry.

Prophets are to labour in a time when the word of the Lord is seemingly rare, and make it common again. Prophets are to train and equip the church to do what comes naturally to them. Since prophets have a grace over their lives to see and hear what God is doing, their function in ministry is to equip others to do the same.

Jesus said something very interesting in Matthew 10:41 (NIV), "Whoever welcomes a prophet as a prophet will receive a prophet's reward." What is the prophet's reward, you ask? A prophet's reward is to see what the Lord is doing and to hear what He is saying. Receiving the ministry of prophets results in the body of Christ being attuned to the voice of God. Therefore, we are all equipped to release God's word in our areas of influence.

The last aspect I'll touch on is that prophets have the ears of the influential to speak the word of the Lord. Prophetic people may prophesy over their family members, co-workers, or people they see out and about, whereas a prophet will be entrusted to speak the word of the Lord to the influential.

In Old Testament times, prophets didn't only speak the word of the Lord to the common Israelite. Many prophets were counsellors of kings. They gave strategy for war. Since they spoke into the ears of the influential, their words had a dramatic impact. The words of prophets would, therefore, impact the masses, nations, and generations. The same could be said of prophets today.

Whether we are a prophet or not, there is a question that we can ask ourselves: Is the word of the Lord rare in our sphere of influence? If it is, then we need to remember that God has called us where we stand for a reason. Remember, you are called as a leader in your sphere. What is God's vision for where you lead? You can be a prophetic voice wherever the Lord has planted you.

God wants to use you to make His word common again in your sphere of influence.

God wants to make His word common in your sphere of influence.

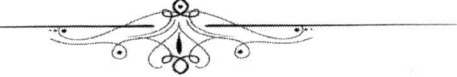

Chapter Twelve
Prophetic Mandate

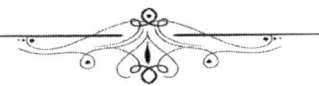

What would it look like if God's word impacted your sphere of influence?

We are living in a remarkable time. All across the world, lives are being transformed by the power and love of God. Bodies are being healed; the tormented are freed. The dead are raised, and those once held in bondage are liberated. All of this is a part of God's strategy so that people throughout the earth are impacted by His boundless love. It is a divine plan woven by His very will—one in which each of us plays a significant role.

In positioning ourselves to be aligned with this move of God, we need to ask ourselves the questions: Where am I called, and how do I partner with God to become a mouthpiece for Him in my sphere of influence?

One of the things I love most about *Royal Identity Academy*, the ministry school my wife and I founded, is that we have the honour of training people from multiple streams of influence. Here are some of the amazing stories from a few of our attendees:

A friend of mine who is involved with our school is a respected business leader. He works in a high position with a specific company in the downtown core. In spending time with the Lord, God asked him to rally the Christians in the company to pray together once per week. After chatting with several believers, word spread like wildfire. Before they knew it, seventy believers were meeting weekly, believing for God to move in businesses in this particular city.

At one meeting, they were interceding for the business realm when the presence of God tangibly came upon them. His presence was so palpable that a literal cloud of God's glory filled the boardroom where they were praying!

He and his colleagues have witnessed remarkable change to their city as the by-product of the kingdom of God invading business. They have accomplished this through prayer, hearing the voice of God, and obedience to what He says.

Another man who attended our school was a schoolteacher, teaching grade four and five students. He implemented several kingdom concepts in his classrooms. He would teach his students to interpret one another's dreams and guide them in receiving prophetic words for one another. One amazing thing that he incorporated into their classroom culture was that whenever someone was sick or in pain, the entire class would pray, believing for healing.

One day, one of the students came to school with a bandage wrapped around his arm. He had severely sprained his arm due to a hockey injury. The students came around him, praying for healing. In the moment, they didn't witness immediate change. Later that night, this boy went to sleep with his arm tightly fastened. When he awoke in the morning, he looked down at his arm, surprised to see that he no longer wore the bandage. He stretched out his hand; his arm was completely healed. He looked over, seeing the bandage folded up on his bedside table!

It turns out that this boy's father was a pastor of a very conservative church. This man emailed the school, writing, "Up until now, I didn't believe that Jesus healed. As of today, I was proven wrong. I now know beyond any shadow of a doubt that Jesus still heals."

Stories such as these light my heart on fire. I love hearing about men, women, and children running full throttle in the things of God. With all my heart, I believe we are living in a time when the pulpit and pew separation is coming to a distinct close. Believing that it is more radical or spiritual to lead from a pulpit compared to leading in business, government, the arts, etc., is a flawed mentality. Many of my friends who challenge me with their radical passion to advance God's kingdom are not in conventional ministry. They stand as beacons of light in business, government, the education system, church, family, arts/entertainment, and media. God is raising up a kingdom army that demonstrates His love in every vein of society.

Every one of us is called to do remarkable things for God's kingdom. Many of you who are reading this book may not be called to have influence with the church as a minister. Perhaps you are called to teach high school students. Maybe you are called to write songs or paint. Perhaps you are a stay-at-home parent or are called to business. No matter where you are called, God has a plan to impact lives through you in your sphere of influence.

I will share one final story with you.

I was ministering at a youth conference in a rural town in Saskatchewan, Canada. Three hundred youth came to listen and receive. I spent time training these teenagers in healing and hearing God's voice. During the gatherings, we saw a mighty outpouring of healing. We saw blind eyes open. Shriveled hands stretched out. Young girls who had self-mutilated their bodies watched as Jesus erased scars up and down their arms right before their very eyes. One after another, we witnessed undeniable miracles. We must have witnessed at least one hundred healings throughout the evening.

A few months after this outpouring, I was speaking at another conference in a nearby area. At the end of ministering, a young fifteen-year-old boy came up to me.

He said, "I was at the conference a few months back."

I knew right away what he was talking about. "You saw all of those healings?" I asked.

He nodded, saying, "I did—and it changed me. I couldn't live my life the same after seeing what I saw."

"How did it change you?" I asked.

The teenager replied, "I was with two friends shortly after. We were playing video games when I felt God speak to me, saying, 'Go to the nearest hospital.'

"I told my friends what I felt like God said to me. We packed up our game and rode our bikes to the hospital. When we arrived, I saw a woman burst through the entrance door. She was fully pregnant and was weeping hysterically.

"I knew she was the reason why we were there. Walking up to her, I asked, 'What's wrong?'

"She replied, saying, 'The doctor just told me that my baby passed away in my womb.'

"I said to her, 'Not long ago, I was at a youth conference where I saw miracles. I've seen Jesus heal. He can heal your baby. Can I pray for you?'

"This woman nodded her head. I laid my hand on her belly and began to pray. I didn't feel anything for my first few times praying, but then I suddenly felt a kick. I then felt another!

"My friends and I came back to the hospital the following day, and we saw the woman again. When she saw us, she gave us a wide smile, saying, 'The doctors are baffled. My baby was risen from the dead in my womb!'"

Isn't Jesus wonderful?! Only He can do something so extravagant.

I'm sure your heart was just as stirred reading that story as mine was writing it. What an amazing God we serve. He's a God who longs to set paths straight. He loves to heal brokenness and ignite hope. The truth is that God doesn't need someone who is *perfect* in order to hear Him. He doesn't need the *polished*. He doesn't need the *flawless*. All He needs is someone with an adamant yes in their heart. He can work with that. With a yielded heart, He can transform lives, homes, communities, cities, and nations.

My friend, you weren't born by random happening— your life is one of far greater importance. You were designed for purpose, born for friendship with the very One who imagined you into being. You were shaped to walk so closely with Him that you hear His faintest of whispers, called to come so near that you will be entrusted with the deep secrets of His heart. You are a child of significance, and you were fashioned for connection with the very heart of God. You were created for impact and legacy.

You, my friend, were born to hear God.

BORN TO HEAR GOD

AN IN-DEPTH LOOK AT THE PROPHETIC MINISTRY

ROYAL IDENTITY ACADEMY

INTERNATIONAL

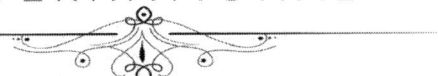

Did you know that you were created for friendship with God? Did you know that you have a remarkable calling and destiny over your life? At Royal Identity Academy we will teach you the keys and kingdom principles required to live out the fullness of who God has created you to be. Thousands have partaken of this school, being trained and equipped in kingdom lifestyle. Royal Identity Academy is an online school designed to fit around your schedule.

We would love to be a part of your journey by having you as a student.

Enrol at **drlucniebergall.com**

More Written Works:

Pioneer is an invitation into understanding the road that is guiding us to our God-given destiny. It's a road that isn't meant to be walked alone but in friendship with God. It's one where we learn about identity, persistence, faith, and how to overcome. Through stories, teaching, and revelation, *Pioneer* shows us how to live a life of longevity, legacy, and—most importantly—friendship with God. We live in a time where God is raising up a people who will demonstrate His goodness and glory to families, communities, cities, nations, and generations. He is raising up pioneers who will influence and transform lives from the place of closeness to His heart.

DRLUCNIEBERGALL.COM

The Heart of Heaven is a prophetic message about friendship with God and identity. These pages consist of a series of dreams and visions that Dr. Luc Niebergall received from the Lord between 2004–2012. God desires for each of us to lay aside the shackles of orphanhood, to embrace our crowns of sonship and daughterhood. This record of dreams and visions is an invitation to embark upon a sacred journey into hope, purpose, and friendship with God.

The Father longs to reveal your true identity.

DRLUCNIEBERGALL.COM

Warrior is a call to stand victoriously as sons and daughters of God. Each of us plays a prominent part in the spiritual war taking place. We have been mandated to bear the light and love of God, dethroning the kingdom of darkness. Through stories, teaching, and revelation, Warrior shows us how to navigate spiritual warfare from rest, victory, and identity in Christ. As sons and daughters of God, victory isn't our destination; it's our dwelling place.

DRLUCNIEBERGALL.COM

Rise of Shadow • Reign of Light Trilogy

Rise of Shadow • Reign of Light is a fiction fantasy trilogy written under Dr. Luc Niebergall's pen name *L.R. Knight*. It is an epic adventure tale brimming with messages of hope, identity, and the kingdom of God. Children, teenagers, and adults alike all throughout North America have enjoyed this enthralling story.

"Stories can speak to the hidden places of our souls. They encourage us to lay aside the complexities of adulthood; to once again embrace childlike wonder." - L.R. Knight

LRKNIGHT.CA

Available Published Works:

Dr. Luc Niebergall

The Heart of Heaven
Pioneer
Born to Hear God
Unlocking the Language of Dreams
Warrior
Adventures in the Glory (with Charlie Robinson)
Revival Secrets (with Samuel Robinson)

L.R. Knight (fiction pen name)

Song of the Dark Lands
Road of a Paragon
A Journey through Fire
The Golden Land

ROYALIDENTITY.CA
LRKNIGHT.CA

Dr. Luc Niebergall lives in Alberta, Canada, with his wife, Sophie. Luc serves as a recognized prophetic voice throughout Canada and the nations. He is the founder of *Royal Identity Academy - International*, which purposes to train people throughout the world in the things of God. He also founded *House of Scribes*, to equip emerging writers and authors. Luc has planted and hosted multiple ministry schools and is sought out to prophetically speak into the lives of influential leaders in government, business, the church, and the arts. Luc is the author of several books in multiple genres. He has been featured on television, radio, and in documentaries. Luc has his doctoral degree in ministry.

Manufactured by Amazon.ca
Bolton, ON

50006370R00129